HISTORY ALIVE 3

1789—1914

Peter Moss

Illustrated by
George B. Hamilton

BLOND EDUCATIONAL

This series, planned to cover the C.S.E. syllabus in depth, gains its delightfully fresh approach by combining a fluid and vivid text with an amusing and highly original style of illustration.

History Alive Source Book
by I. Bereson and W. Lamb
120pp   219.51602.2

Containing relevant documentary material to supplement the Course Books, this book covers numerous readings and exercises in British History from 1485 to the present.

Lives
by Neil Grant

These books for top primary and lower secondary classes provide additional biographical material, illustrated in the vein of the main series.

ACKNOWLEDGEMENT
The author and publisher wish to thank Longmans Green and Co. for permission to quote the extract from *Garibaldi and the Making of Italy*, by G. M. Trevelyan.

Reprinted 1969, 1970, 1972

Series cover design by Lyon Benzimra

First published in Great Britain 1968 by Blond Educational, Iliffe House, Iliffe Avenue, Oadby, Leicester, LE2 4ZB. © Copyright 1968 Peter Moss. Illustrations © Copyright 1968 Blond Educational. Made and printed in Great Britain at the Pitman Press, Bath.

219.51636.7

Contents

CHANGES THE INDUSTRIAL REVOLUTION MADE IN BRITAIN, 1750-1900

FARMING   INDUSTRY

HOME MANUFACTURES   FACTORIES

VILLAGE   CITY

MUSCLE   MACHINERY

SMALL ISLAND

CHIEF WORLD POWER

POPULATION, 10,000,000   30,000,000

5 m.p.h.   60 m.p.h.

POVERTY   POWER

1

THE INDUSTRIAL REVOLUTION

The story of Britain in the years 1789-1900 is largely the story of the Industrial Revolution—that is, how Britain changed from being an agricultural country to an industrial one. This diagram shows the changes in agricultural and industrial output between 1801 and 1901.

Changes in the amount of money received by agriculture and industry in the nineteenth century.

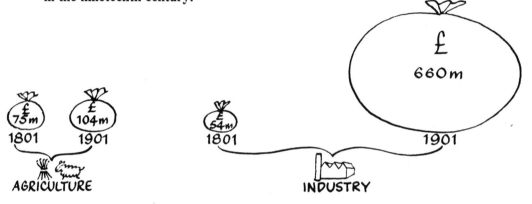

£75m 1801   £104m 1901

AGRICULTURE

£54m 1801   £660m 1901

INDUSTRY

This is the century when wood gave way to iron and steel, and when muscle power was replaced by steam power. These were the years when the manufacture of all kinds of goods moved from simple hand machines in people's homes to huge, powered machines in gigantic factories. These were the years when great industrial cities sprang up in the midlands and north of England and Scotland; in which horse-drawn waggons lumbering along muddy roads at 3 miles an hour gave way to express trains rushing along a network of railways at 60 miles an hour, and in which the population rose from a mere 10 millions to 30 millions.

    These were the years of science, discovery and invention; of slums, disease and plague. This was the age of the struggle of the working people for education, freedom and a decent standard of living. These were the years that made Britain the richest, most powerful and most advanced country in the world, importing food and raw materials from every corner of the globe and more than paying for them by exporting

5

vast quantities of every type of manufactured product from drawing pins to sea-going liners. These charts give some idea of Britain's position in the world at the end of the nineteenth century.

The world's merchant shipping in 1890.

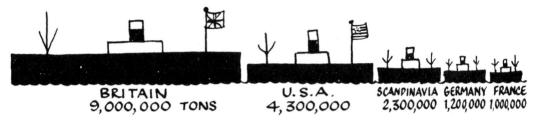

| BRITAIN | U.S.A. | SCANDINAVIA | GERMANY | FRANCE |
| 9,000,000 TONS | 4,300,000 | 2,300,000 | 1,200,000 | 1,000,000 |

Trade (exports and imports) for 1880 and 1890.

BRITAIN £1,443,000,000

GERMANY £860,000

FRANCE £640,000

Town and country dwellers.
Of every ten people the following lived in towns.

BRITAIN

FRANCE

U.S.A.

GERMANY

Why the Industrial Revolution took place

The Industrial Revolution was the greatest change that had ever taken place in British history—or indeed in the history of the modern world, because Britain became industrialised almost 50 years before any other country. The explosion shook the nation to its very foundations and turned its whole way of life upside down. Even today, over a century later, the effects of this great upheaval are still being felt in our housing,

6

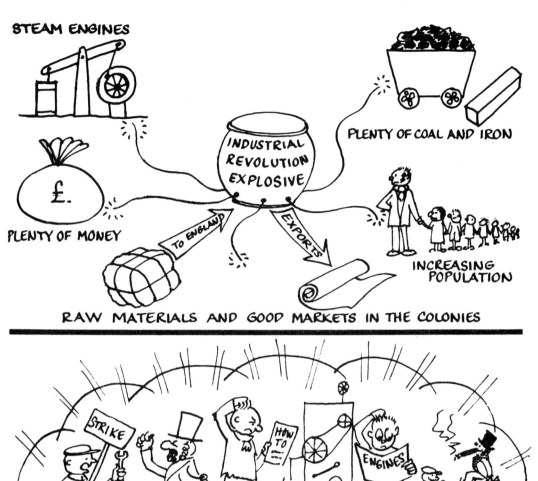

STEAM ENGINES

PLENTY OF COAL AND IRON

INDUSTRIAL REVOLUTION EXPLOSIVE

PLENTY OF MONEY

£.

TO ENGLAND

EXPORTS

INCREASING POPULATION

RAW MATERIALS AND GOOD MARKETS IN THE COLONIES

STRIKE

WAGES

NEED FOR EDUCATION

ENGINES

RISE OF TRADE UNIONS

INDUSTRIAL REVOLUTION EXPLOSION

OPPORTUNITIES FOR WEALTH

£

M.P.

NEED FOR CHANGES IN PARLIAMENT

CITY SLUMS AND DISEASE

RISING STANDARD OF LIVING

our transport systems, our attitude to industry and our position in the world.

During the seventeenth and eighteenth centuries Britain had won many colonies such as India, Canada and much of America until 1783. As many of these countries were undeveloped they urgently needed manufactured goods of all kinds, especially cloth and small metal items. In return Britain could obtain raw materials such as cotton very cheaply from them.

Many merchants, especially the slave dealers, were very wealthy, and were anxious to invest their money to make even more. They were willing to pour large sums into new businesses, factories and inventions if these looked like showing a good profit.

There was, therefore, a great demand for goods, and many business men were anxious to make them, but these reasons alone might not have been enough if the population had not risen so sharply in the eighteenth and nineteenth centuries. All of these extra people had to be fed and clothed, and work had to be found for them. The new methods of farming introduced between 1700 and 1800 needed fewer labourers so that there were large numbers of unemployed country men and women, who were desperate to find work.

The old system of hand manufacture could not absorb all of these extra people, but just at the right moment there came a number of inventions which changed the whole picture. The Darby family discovered ways of producing iron cheaply and in large quantities: Kay, Hargreaves, Arkwright and Crompton invented machines to speed up weaving and spinning, and James Watt improved the clumsy steam engine so that it could drive the new machinery efficiently.

Yet all of this might have come to little if Britain had not had vast seams of coal and iron waiting to be mined. As it was, everything was in its right place at the right time: the demand for cloth, the money, the inventors, the coal and iron, and the workers. The five pieces of the jig-saw fitted perfectly, and the Industrial Revolution was under way.

The coming of the steam engine

Without a doubt the one invention that made the Industrial Revolution possible was that of an efficient steam engine to replace machines driven by human muscles, horses or water power.

As early as 1705 Thomas Newcomen had invented a crude steam engine for pumping water from the Cornish tin mines, but this worked very slowly and used an enormous amount of coal. In addition it produced only an up and down movement which was quite suitable for pumping but could not be used to drive other machinery.

8

About 1760 James Watt was asked to repair a model of Newcomen's engine and he realised at once that he could improve it. He produced the simple but revolutionary device you can see in Fig 2, and by 1780

Newcomen's steam engine.

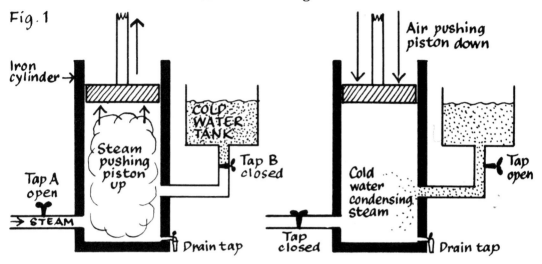

To start, tap **B** was closed and tap **A** opened to let the steam push the piston upwards. When this was at the top, tap **A** was closed to shut off the steam and tap **B** opened to let cold water into the cylinder to condense the steam. The air then pushed the piston back down. Unfortunately the cold water also cooled the heavy iron cylinder which had to be heated again before the steam could start to push up the piston for the second stroke. This wasted a great deal of fuel.

The secret of James Watt's engine.

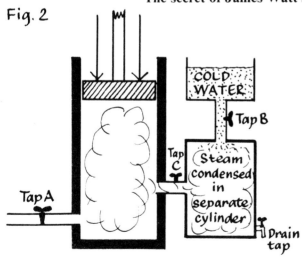

Watt's great invention was very simple. When the piston reached the top of its stroke, tap **A** closed to shut off the steam. Tap **C** then opened to let the steam escape from the main cylinder into a *separate* cylinder by the side. Cold water was let into this second cylinder to condense the steam. By this means the main cylinder was not cooled as in the Newcomen engine, and the piston was ready for the next stroke immediately. This saved so much fuel that for every ton of coal burned by a Newcomen engine, a Watt engine used only five hundredweights.

9

he had a factory turning out engines which were faster and more powerful than Newcomen's, and also used less than one quarter of the coal. In addition, Watt invented a way of making his engines turn a large wheel which could be used to drive machines such as spinning jennies. This was all that was needed to set the Industrial Revolution sweeping through the land. Long before 1800 the steam engine was pumping water and lifting cages in coal mines, working bellows and great hammers in iron works and turning machinery in factories of all kinds.

Such an engine was obviously going to be used in transport, too, and by 1812 the first serious steamship and goods railway were in operation (see Chapter 2).

All through the nineteenth century engineers improved and re-designed the steam engine to make it more powerful and more efficient until Watt would scarcely have recognised his own invention. There were steam cranes, steam ploughs, steam road trucks and even attempts to make steam flying machines. For over a hundred years steam was king, for it was the steam engine that had made Britain the richest and most powerful country in the world. British trains and British ships carried goods made in British factories all over the world—and all of these depended on the steam engine.

Then, suddenly, in fifteen years, came three developments which in the twentieth century were to unseat steam as the king of power. In 1870 scientists working in Italy, Belgium and France discovered how to make electricity in a practicable way using a dynamo. This obviously had a great future, but it was not a success until Sir William Parsons invented the turbine in 1884. This was still driven by steam but it was a completely different machine from the old Watt-type engine, and as it ran very smoothly and at high speed it was ideal for driving dynamos and ships. About the same time Dr Daimler in Germany perfected the petrol engine which now powers cars, buses, ships and aeroplanes all over the world. By the end of the nineteenth century, however, all three of these great discoveries were only just coming into serious use.

The effects of steam power

The coming of steam power to replace hand labour was bound to have a great effect on the lives of the people. First of all, the engines were very big and expensive and could not be bought by ordinary people to drive their spinning wheels or simple machinery at home. Wealthy merchants built huge sheds, installed machines in them and powered these by steam. Instead of working at home as they had done in the past, people were forced to go to the new factories as they could no longer make enough money on their slow hand machines.

As the steam-driven equipment worked so much harder and faster

SOME OF THE EFFECTS OF THE STEAM ENGINE

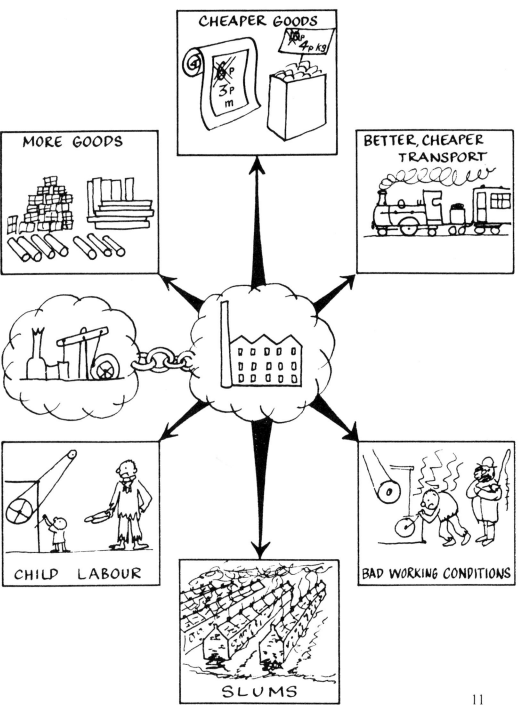

than hand machines, many more goods were produced by the same number of workers. This not only meant that prices began to fall but also that more people could enjoy them. At the end of the century ordinary working families had clothes, furniture, carpets, ornaments, books, food, amusements and many comforts which a hundred years earlier would have been beyond the dreams of anyone except a very rich man.

The steam-driven railways and ships made transport faster, more comfortable and much cheaper so that ordinary people could now travel. Before the Industrial Revolution few men went more than ten miles from their birthplace in the whole of their lives, but now they could travel far and wide seeking work, visiting relatives or even just for pleasure. The faster transport enabled perishable foods such as milk, vegetables, fruit, meat and fish to be moved quickly from the country or coast to the towns so that even poor people could now enjoy them. In the end the steam engine caused the standard of living to rise in every direction, but to millions of working people in the first half of the nineteenth century it seemed to bring nothing but evil.

Before the Industrial Revolution much of industry had depended on muscle power. Women and children were not strong enough for working with iron, for example, nor even for the heavy hand looms, so that these had to be managed by men. Now, under the factory system, steam supplied the power and a woman or even a child could pull a lever or turn a knob to make the machine work as easily as a man could—and a child could be paid less than a quarter of a man's wage. As a result wages were very low, and often the whole family—father, mother and all the children over three or four years old—had to work in the factory or mine for twelve or more hours a day in order to earn enough to live.

Although when people worked in their own homes the hours were long and the work hard, they were their own masters and could stop when they felt like a break. In the factory they were forced to keep moving as long as the engine kept pounding, and there are many reports of children collapsing from sheer weariness into the machines. The factories were often very hot, badly ventilated and full of fumes and fluff. Many of the factory owners were so harsh and greedy that if any worker stopped for a drink or to open a window he was often fined as much as half a day's wages.

Life in the factory was bad, and life outside was, for much of the century, little better. The workers usually lived in rows of tiny, poorly-built hovels which clustered round the factory itself. These over-crowded, rat-infested, filthy streets soon became the worst slums in Europe, as you can read in Chapter 4. The working people of the early Industrial Revolution paid a terrible price for the comforts and prosperity they were to bring to later generations.

The cottage system.

The merchant collected the wool . . . took it to the spinners and collected the yarn they had spun. He took the yarn to the weavers' cottages and took away the cloth they had woven. This method was slow and led to great variation in quality because some workers were much better than others.

The factory system.

The merchant installed all the spinning machines in a huge shed and powered them first by water wheels, and later by steam engines. He could now keep an eye on his workers, but for them it was almost slavery.

Although we tend to think of steam engines driving machines in factories, railways and steamships, they were tried in many other fields. There were steam airships, steam aeroplanes (which did not really fly), steam roundabouts, steam organs, steam cranes, steam cars, steam tractors, steam motorcycles, and even a steam submarine in 1879.

How industry moved during the Industrial Revolution following the coal which was needed for the steam engine.

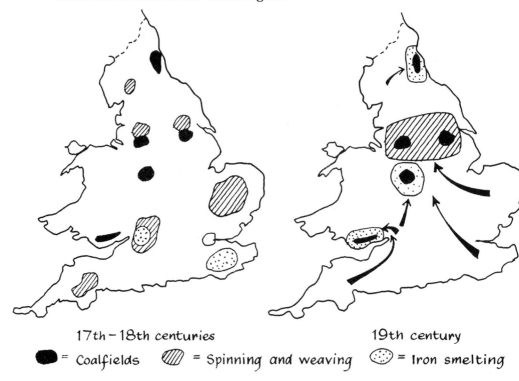

17th – 18th centuries   19th century

● = Coalfields   ▨ = Spinning and weaving   ⊙ = Iron smelting

Before the industrial revolution, in the days of the cottage industry, spinning and weaving took place all over the country, but East Anglia, Gloucester, Somerset and Wiltshire, parts of Devon, Cumberland, Lancashire and Yorkshire were especially well known. After the steam engine and the factory system became widespread there was little textile industry except in Lancashire (mainly cotton) and Yorkshire (mainly wool). The main iron smelting areas moved from Sussex and Gloucestershire to the coal fields of Wales, the midlands and the north east.

Coal mining

Until the eighteenth century there was little demand for coal in Britain. A small amount was used for heating the vats in making beer and soap, and some was used in houses in the towns where it was difficult to get wood. But as the majority of the population still lived in the countryside, timber was the chief fuel for all purposes.

The mines, therefore, were small and shallow, and the coal was brought to the surface in baskets either carried on men's backs or hauled up by horse-driven windlasses. On the surface the roads from the pithead to the nearest port or customer were usually too bad for carts so that the loads had to be carried by packhorses. As each animal could carry only a few hundredweights at a time, moving coal in any quantity was a slow and expensive business.

Suddenly in the eighteenth century the demand for coal soared. In 1730 a method of smelting iron with coke instead of wood charcoal was discovered, and as timber was already becoming scarce in iron districts, large quantities of coal began to be used. After 1780 Watt's steam engine began to be used more and more in industry and this once more pushed up the demand for coal. During the nineteenth century railways, steamships, factories and gas works all needed fuel in ever-increasing amounts.

The tiny pits and the slow, lumbering packhorses could no longer supply enough to meet the new needs, and mines had to be made deeper and deeper to reach the bigger, richer seams that lay below. But with every yard downwards fresh problems arose. Water began to flood the workings; dangerous gases leaked into the tunnels; it was so far to the surface that the coal could no longer be carried by men or by horse windlass. Finally, at the great depths the danger of passages collapsing increased alarmingly.

Transport on the surface was the first of the problems to be solved. By the middle of the eighteenth century canals were being built to carry coal cheaply and quickly from the mines to the ports and to some inland towns. The railways came into use early in the nineteenth century (see Chapter 2), carrying coal more quickly than the barges and to places where the canals could not reach.

Almost as soon as it was invented the Watt steam engine was seized on by the colliery owners for pumping water from the pits and for hauling coal up the shafts. A little later iron cages and wire ropes were introduced to make transport to the surface quicker and safer.

Better pumps and lifting gear tempted mine owners to make their pits deeper still so that the problem of ventilation rapidly grew worse. One gas suffocated the miners and another, much more dangerous, was so highly explosive that a single spark could destroy a whole pit. In 1805 Sir Humphrey Davy invented a safety lamp which allowed the miners to have a glimmer of light at the coal face without the danger of explosion, but mine owners made this an excuse to make their pits deeper still. As a result the number of deaths rose: there were fewer from explosions but the increase in those from rock falls more than made up for this.

The only real answer to the gas problem was good ventilation. The powerful fans which are used today had not been invented so that the best that could be done was to dig two shafts to each pit. At the bottom of one a huge fire was lit and the hot air rising from this drew fresh air down the other and through the tunnels. To make sure the clean air

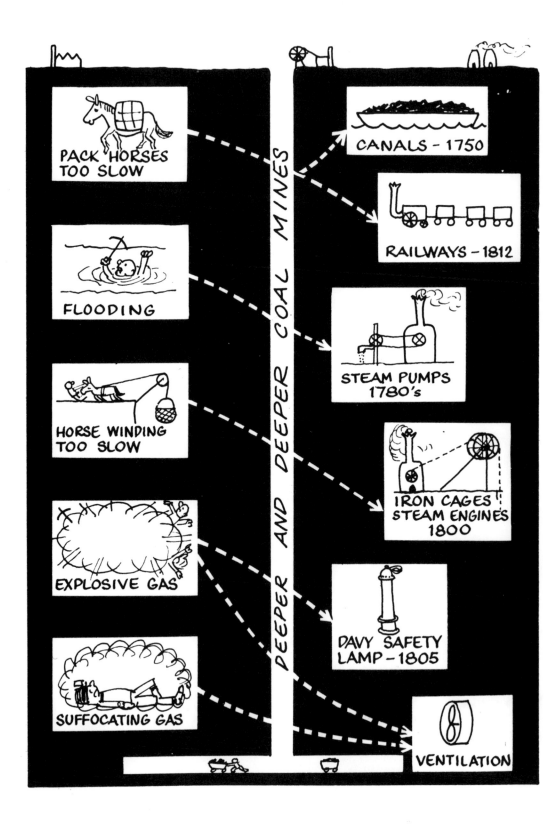

How fresh air was sent round the mine workings. In sketch **B** a door has been left open to show how the clean air could take a short cut and allow gas to accumulate.

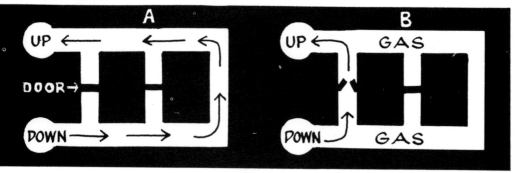

passed through all of the passages doors were fixed across any side galleries.

Opening and closing these doors when a tub of coal was being pushed along the tunnel was the job of children often only four years old. As you see in the drawing above, failure to close even one door could lead to an explosion which would kill hundreds of people. And this responsible job was left to mere babies working in pitch darkness hundreds of feet below the ground. This is what two of these children said to the government inspectors in 1842:

"I'm a trapper in the Gamber Pit. I have to trap without a light and I'm scared. I go at four and sometimes half-past three in the morning and come out at five and half-past. I never go to sleep. Sometimes I sing when I've a light, but not in the dark . . . "

"I been down almost three years [that is, when he was $4\frac{1}{2}$]. When I first went down I couldn't keep my eyes open; I don't fall asleep now; I smokes my pipe . . . "

17

How coal production rose

1700	1800	1850	1899
ABOUT 2 MILLION TONS	ABOUT 10 MILLION TONS	49 MILLION TONS	220 MILLION TONS

As you can see in the drawing here above five times as much coal was produced in 1850 as in 1800, and by 1899 over twenty times as much was being mined. To give some idea of what 220,000,000 tons of coal means, imagine it all loaded on 5-ton lorries. If these trucks were placed nose to tail they would stretch in an unbroken line for 200,000 miles—eight times round the earth. This tremendous amount could not have been produced without the great improvements in the workings underground which came in the second half of the century.

The steam engine which was so useful for hauling coal to the surface and for pumping out water was at a disadvantage underground. Its smoke would add to the ventilation problem and, more serious, there was the danger of setting fire to the gases. Nevertheless, some pits did instal engines at the bottom of the shafts to pull trucks along the tunnels by means of long ropes. Until the 1840s however, most mines still employed women and children to drag the tubs of coal from the face to the shaft. When this was forbidden by law in 1842 ponies were used wherever the size of the tunnel allowed it.

Soon after the middle of the century steam-driven fans on the surface were used to suck out stale air and drive fresh down. This enabled pits to be made deeper and further afield, but it increased the problems of haulage underground.

The first big advance in this direction came in 1880 when locomotives driven by compressed air were used to pull trains of tubs along the tunnels. These were safe and fast but they were liable to run out of air at inconvenient places. At about the same time the first experiments were made with electric lights underground and a few lucky miners even had portable lamps. These, however, were extremely rare and the Davy safety lamps were general for the next thirty or forty years.

With the coming of electricity it was obvious that here was the perfect answer for underground haulage. In the 1890s huge electric motors were installed in a few pits to pull the tubs by means of wire

18

Later developments in the mines.

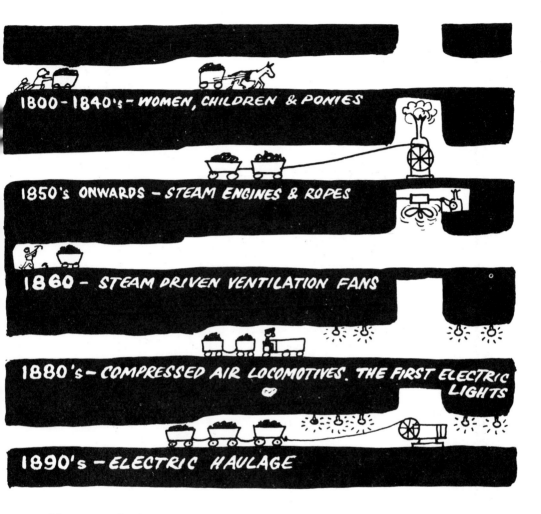

1800 - 1840's - WOMEN, CHILDREN & PONIES

1850's ONWARDS - STEAM ENGINES & ROPES

1860 - STEAM DRIVEN VENTILATION FANS

1880's - COMPRESSED AIR LOCOMOTIVES. THE FIRST ELECTRIC LIGHTS

1890's - ELECTRIC HAULAGE

Note—even in the 1950s thousands of ponies were still used in the coal mines.

ropes, some of them several miles long. Electricity too, seemed the perfect way of replacing the miner's pick and shovel, and a rush of inventions for mechanical cutting and digging machinery appeared. By the end of the century these were still in their infancy and almost all of that incredible weight of over two hundred million tons was hacked out by human muscle power.

HOW THE TEXTILE INDUSTRY SPARKED OFF THE INDUSTRIAL REVOLUTION

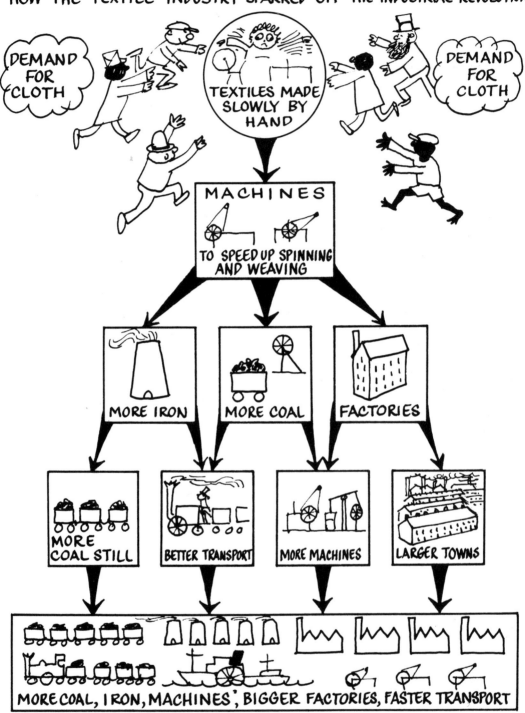

Textile manufacture

At the beginning of the eighteenth century the making of cloth was very little quicker than it had been in Roman times. It is true that the spinning wheel had speeded up the making of yarn a little, but the looms on which this thread was woven into cloth had scarcely changed in eighteen hundred years.

By 1700 the colonists in North America, the slave merchants trading to Africa and the people of the East were demanding so much cloth that the hand spinners and weavers could no longer keep pace with their simple equipment. In the last three-quarters of the eighteenth century many new machines were invented to speed up the manufacture of textiles which solved the problem of demand but created a great many difficulties the inventors had never dreamed of. More machines needed more iron: more iron needed more coal; the machines had to be placed in factories. More iron and more coal meant better transport and more machines to mine coal and smelt the iron. Factories meant more people in one place so that houses had to be built . . . which meant yet more transport, which meant more iron, more coal and more machines. The whole thing went in a steep spiral which we call the Industrial Revolution.

In the manufacture of textiles, either by hand or by machine, there are two main processes by which wool or cotton is turned into cloth. These are spinning and weaving.

Spinning

The tangled wool or cotton . . .   is combed out straight . . .   and is then twisted together to make a thread, or yarn.

Weaving

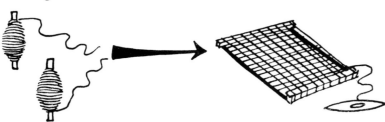

Two or more sets of yarn . . .   are criss-crossed on a loom to make cloth.

How the balance changed.

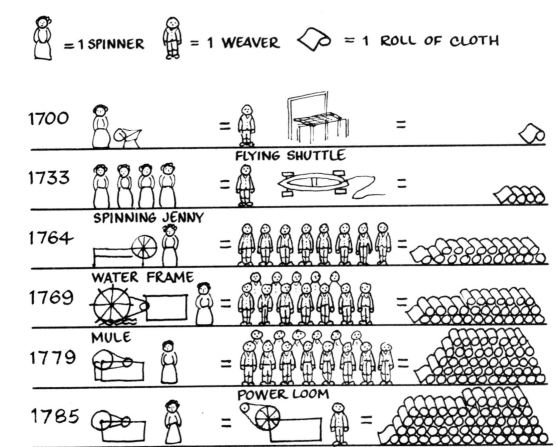

In the early eighteenth century the spinning was normally done by women and girls on a spinning wheel, and the weaving by men on a hand loom. One spinner could usually make just enough yarn to keep one weaver busy, and the upsetting of this one-spinner-one-weaver balance was one of the main causes of the Industrial Revolution. Here are the main inventions in the textile industry.

1733 John Kay's Flying Shuttle. This simple device enabled a weaver to make four times as much cloth on his loom. The cloth was not only woven more quickly, but could also be made wider.

1764 Hargreaves' Spinning Jenny. This was a new kind of spinning wheel which spun up to 80 threads at a time instead of one. (See page 26).

1769 Arkwright's Water Frame. This was another spinning invention which was driven by a water wheel. It spun faster than the Jenny and made a stronger, thinner thread.

1779 Crompton's Mule. This was another spinning invention which was a cross between the Jenny and the Water Frame but which was better than either. This was often powered by a steam engine.

1785 Cartwright's power loom. This was the first important weaving invention since the Flying Shuttle. It was driven by a steam engine and could use all of the yarn spun by one mule.

Notice that in 1700 one spinner could spin enough yarn on a hand wheel to keep one weaver busy on a hand loom. In 1805 one spinner working steam-driven jennies could still make enough yarn to keep one weaver on a power loom busy, but they would produce about fifty times as much cloth as the hand workers.

When the Flying Shuttle was invented the SPINNERS were delighted because all of the weavers wanted more and more yarn. This meant the spinners were always busy and could put up their prices.

When the Jenny and other spinning machines were invented it was the WEAVERS who were pleased. There was so much yarn being spun that they could bargain and force prices down. This meant that the weavers became richer and richer, while the spinners became desperately poor. Many of them, working as fast as they could for twelve or more hours a day, seven days a week, would earn less than 50p. The spinners blamed the machines for their poverty and many of them went from house to house and sometimes factory to factory, smashing the jennies and water frames.

The government passed very strict laws against the machine smashers as this extract from *The Liverpool Mercury* of April 25th, 1817, shows.

"Leicester, April 17th. The most melancholy spectacle ever witnessed at Leicester took place this day, in the execution of seven men under sentence of death, viz. the six Luddites [a gang of men who broke up machines] for destroying lace machines . . . in the factory of Messrs Heathcote and Boden, at Loughborough last June . . . As early as six o'clock in the morning they were removed, under military escort, from the jail to the new Bridewell, to be executed on the new drop. Many thousands of spectators kept assembling until noon, to witness this truly tragic scene, and conducted themselves in the most peaceable manner."

When the power loom was invented in 1785 the tables were turned and now the hand-loom workers could not keep pace with the steam-driven machines in the factories. Those who refused to enter the mills and continued to work in their own homes on the hand loom found themselves slaving for longer and longer hours for less and less money. By 1835, the weavers who thirty years earlier had been among the highest paid workmen and able, as one said, to have meat every day AND butter AND tea, were toiling for up to eighteen hours a day for 25 or 30 pence a week. Hundreds died of sheer starvation and those who managed to survive usually worked and lived in conditions like these, described in 1840:

"I have seen them [the hand-loom workers] working in cellars dug out of an undrained swamp; the streets formed by their houses without sewers, and flooded with rain; the water therefore running down the bare walls of the cellars and rendering them unfit for the abode of dogs or rats. The floor to these cellars is but seldom boarded or paved: a proper place for coals or ashes, but less fitted for a workshop than even an Irish hovel, because underground."

Weavers' wages

1804
£1.33
A WEEK

1818
73p
A WEEK

1834
27p
A WEEK

The two most important textile inventions.

In an ordinary hand-loom, the weaver had to pass the shuttle **S** from hand to hand. This meant he could not weave very wide cloth.

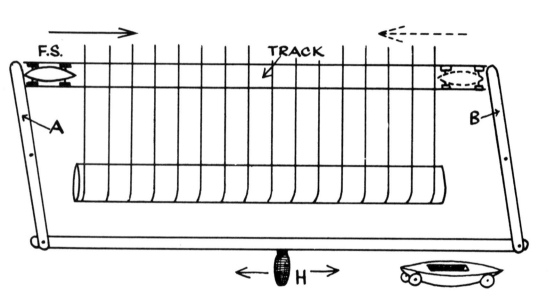

The Flying Shuttle

The flying shuttle had four small wheels and ran on a track across the threads. The weaver jerked the handle **H** to the left which made the arm **A** hit the shuttle. This shot across the threads (warp) dragging the cross thread (weft) with it until it was stopped by the arm **B**. The handle was then jerked to the right and the shuttle was knocked back to its original position. This obviously enabled the weaving to be done much more quickly and allowed a wider cloth to be made.

The great secret of the Industrial Revolution—the Spinning Jenny.

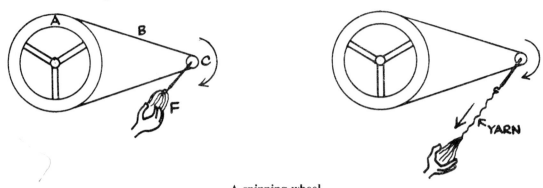

A spinning wheel

A handful of combed fibre **F** was hooked into the notch on the end of the spindle **C**. When the large wheel **A** was turned, the belt **B** caused the spindle to revolve at high speed. At the same time the bundle of fibre was drawn backwards so that a thin twisted yarn was formed. When the fibre was moved towards the machine again, the yarn wrapped itself round the spindle.

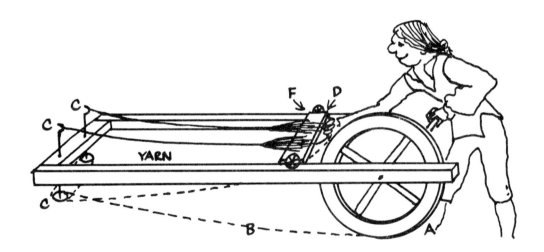

The Spinning Jenny

The Jenny was really a spinning wheel with more than one spindle, and lying on its side. The combed fibres **F** were fixed to a little carriage which moved backwards and forwards on wheels. The spinner moved this carriage right forward and hooked the fibres into the notches on the spindles **C**—only two are shown but some jennies had 120. When the large wheel **A** was turned the belt **B** revolved the spindles. At the same time the spinner pulled the carriage **D** back, so pulling out a thread. When he pushed the carriage forward again the yarn wrapped itself round the spindles and the fibres were ready for pulling out once more.

26

Some other textile inventions

Although the most important inventions were in spinning and weaving, these alone would not have been enough. For example, when cotton has been woven it is a plain grey or brown in colour. Before it can be used it has to be bleached—that is, made white. Until the middle of the eighteenth century this process of bleaching took from three to six months.

First of all the cloth was soaked in strong soda for a week. Then it was spread on the grass in the sunlight for several months, all the time being kept damp. Finally, it was soaked for another week in sour milk.

BLEACHING

SODA — 1 WEEK   SUNLIGHT 2-3 MONTHS   SOUR MILK — 1 WEEK

CHLORINE

BERTHOLLET'S BLEACHING — A FEW HOURS

In 1786 a Frenchman, Berthollet, discovered that the gas chlorine would bleach cloth in a few hours. The cotton was soaked in water in which chlorine had been dissolved or else treated with chloride of lime, a powder containing the gas.

Printing

When cotton has been bleached it is, of course, pure white. While this is suitable for such articles as sheets, for most purposes it needs to be printed with a coloured pattern. Until the middle of the eighteenth century this was done by hand, with large wooden blocks like lino-prints.

Naturally this method was very slow indeed, especially if several colours were needed, as each had to be pressed on separately. For every square yard of cloth the block had to be hammered on sixteen times for each colour.

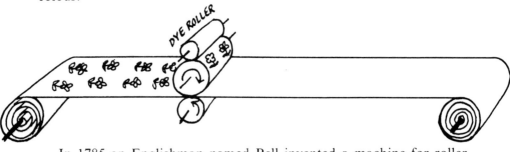

In 1785 an Englishman named Bell invented a machine for roller printing. The pattern was engraved on a copper cylinder which rubbed against a roller soaked with dye. As the cloth ran through the cylinder, rather like clothes through a wringer, the pattern was printed. If more than one colour was needed, there was a separate roller for each and the cloth ran through them one after another. One roller might have flowers engraved on it and would press against a red dye and the next one would have the stem and leaves and would press against a green dye. Roller printing could colour hundreds of yards of material an hour.

These two charts give some idea of how the cotton industry grew in the nineteenth century.

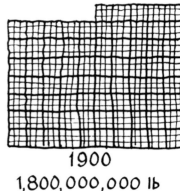
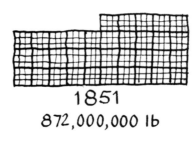

1795	1851	1900
26,000,000 lb	872,000,000 lb	1,800,000,000 lb

Exports of Textiles

1795	1851	1900
2,000,000	£ 32,000,000	£ 67,000,000

Iron and steel

Although Britain had plenty of ore waiting to be quarried, very little iron was actually produced until the eighteenth century. In 1740, for example, all the furnaces in the country together made only 17,000 tons of pig iron—that is, a heap forty feet long, forty wide and forty high. Wood was still the chief material for building and industry and even gear wheels for many machines were made of timber with wooden pegs for teeth.

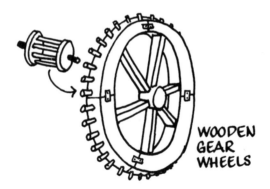

WOODEN GEAR WHEELS

But wooden machinery was so clumsy and slow that if industry was to develop there had to be more iron, cheaper iron and better iron. Many of the great inventions of the eighteenth and nineteenth centuries were aimed at producing this, and their success can be judged by the next chart which shows the production of pig iron in Britain between 1740 and 1899.

At the beginning of the eighteenth century pig iron was made by

Pig iron production

2,500,000 TONS

12,000,000 TONS

110,000 TONS

17,000 TONS

1740   1800   1850   1899

setting fire to a mixture of ore and charcoal (which gave a hotter flame than coal) in a furnace and then blowing in air from a water-driven bellows. When the furnace was hot enough the ore melted to give CAST iron. This could be run off into moulds of any shape, but unfortunately it was very brittle and would not bend. It had, therefore, to be used mainly for large, solid and rather heavy objects such as rollers, pillars, weights and rather clumsy machinery.

If the cast iron was re-melted and treated in a special furnace it could be turned into WROUGHT iron. This process was fairly expensive but it was considered worthwhile because wrought iron could be hammered and twisted into shape and it did not break as easily as cast. Much more accurate machines could now be made but unfortunately wrought iron was not very hard and would not take an edge for tools or weapons. However, for nearly a century it was the best material that the engineers of the industrial revolution had in any quantity.

By melting wrought iron yet once again and putting it through a long, tedious and expensive process, steel could be made, but only in small amounts. Steel is much harder than wrought iron, but at the same time it is much more flexible and can be sharpened and toughened so that it is ideal for tools and fine machines. Because of its high cost (five times the price of wrought iron) for most of the nineteenth century it was kept for making knives, tools, weapons and other engineering equipment in which strength and hardness were essential.

By the beginning of the eighteenth century wood for charcoal was becoming scarce in the iron-smelting districts. There was plenty of coal available in Britain but although many people had tried to use it in the manufacture of iron, no-one had succeeded. About 1730 however, Abraham Darby discovered that if he used coke instead of coal, the ore could be smelted quite satisfactorily. At once the foundries and furnaces moved from the forest areas of Sussex and Gloucestershire to the coal-

30

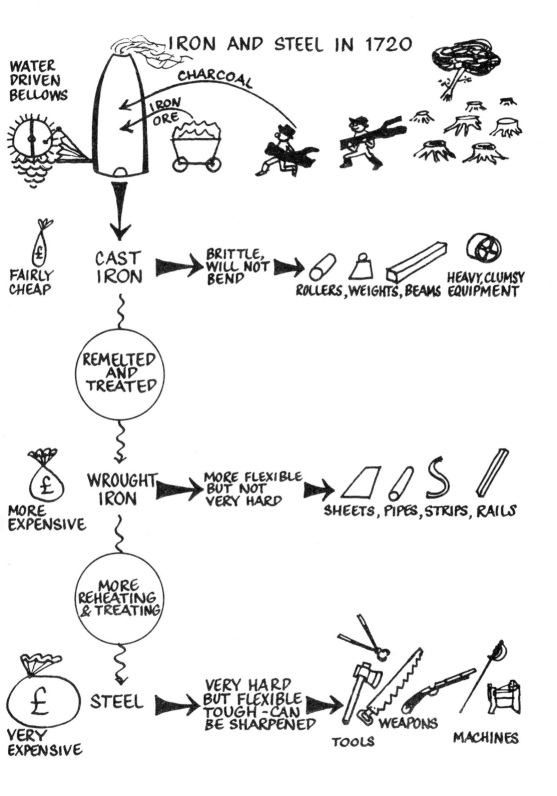

IRON AND STEEL IN 1720

WATER DRIVEN BELLOWS

CHARCOAL

IRON ORE

FAIRLY CHEAP — CAST IRON → BRITTLE, WILL NOT BEND → ROLLERS, WEIGHTS, BEAMS HEAVY, CLUMSY EQUIPMENT

REMELTED AND TREATED

MORE EXPENSIVE — WROUGHT IRON → MORE FLEXIBLE BUT NOT VERY HARD → SHEETS, PIPES, STRIPS, RAILS

MORE REHEATING & TREATING

VERY EXPENSIVE — STEEL → VERY HARD BUT FLEXIBLE TOUGH - CAN BE SHARPENED → TOOLS WEAPONS MACHINES

fields of the midlands and north. Coal was reasonably cheap there and by a fortunate coincidence the iron ore was often found near the mines, so that the price of iron fell sharply.

Unfortunately Darby's process gave only cast iron. It was wrought iron and steel that the industrial revolution really needed, and these were still expensive. The next big advance came in 1784 when Henry Cort invented a method of making large quantities of wrought iron at a reasonable price. To do this molten cast iron was poured into a special 'puddling' furnace and stirred with something which looked like a huge long-handled spoon. The increased supply gave a great boost to engineering, but the steel which would have made things even better, was still scarce and expensive.

All through the nineteenth century scientists, inventors and engineers turned their efforts to improving the quality of iron and to increasing its output. Neilson discovered that by blowing hot air into the furnaces he could use powdered coal instead of having to make coke first. Nasmith invented a gigantic steam hammer for beating out the iron ingots. Maudsley, Wilkinson and many others produced lathes, borers and machine tools of all kinds for shaping the finished metal.

Railways, locomotives, bridges, buildings, machinery, cranes, warships (most merchant ships were made of wood until the last quarter of the century) and a thousand other industrial items were understandably made of iron. But the craze did not stop there. Pillars, ceilings, decorations, ornaments, furniture and even coffins were made of it. It is little wonder that the Victorian period is sometimes called the Age of Iron. Yet all the time the engineers knew that even wrought iron was not the material they wanted, and they longed for a way of making cheap steel. Then suddenly in 1856 Henry Bessemer found an answer with his 'converter'. He took a huge container full of white-hot liquid iron and blew through the bottom a blast of hot air. With an ear-splitting roar a jet of flame shot a hundred feet into the air. When it had burnt itself out Bessemer added a few chemicals to the swirling molten mass and the container was full of steel.

There were still many problems to be overcome but on the whole steel could now be produced almost as cheaply as iron, and engineering took a great leap forward into the twentieth century. (See page 34.)

---

1. Britain became industrialised 50 years before any other country. What advantages were gained from this? In what ways did the industrial revolution help to make Britain a truly great power? (As you try to think about the answer to this question, consider such things as trade, imports, exports, money, colonisation, etc. You may find other things that need consideration also.)

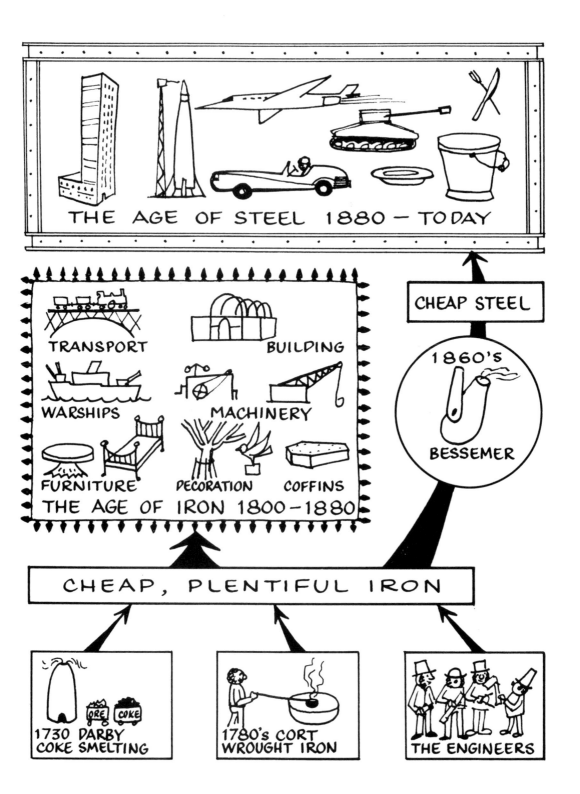

THE AGE OF STEEL 1880 — TODAY

CHEAP STEEL

1860'S

BESSEMER

TRANSPORT
BUILDING
WARSHIPS
MACHINERY
FURNITURE
DECORATION
COFFINS
THE AGE OF IRON 1800—1880

CHEAP, PLENTIFUL IRON

1730 DARBY
COKE SMELTING

1780's CORT
WROUGHT IRON

THE ENGINEERS

2. In your own words explain how the Industrial Revolution got under way. What caused it? What were the results?
3. Explain why steam power had such a major part to play in the Industrial Revolution.
4. Read once again the section on the coming of the steam engine and say, in your own words what was meant by the phrase 'Steam was King.'
5. Explain simply why the arrival of steam power kept wages low.
6. With the aid of history books and encyclopaedias find out what you can about *one* of the following and write a short account of his work and the effect it had on industry:
   Newcomen; James Watt; Kay; Hargreaves; Arkwright; Crompton.
   Illustrate your account if you like.
7. What problems had to be faced in the coal industry once the demand for coal began to increase so rapidly, and what steps were taken to solve them?
8. Which invention do you think most helped the textile industry at this time? Say why you think this.
9. With the aid of an encyclopaedia find out the difference between cast iron, wrought iron and steel.
10. Look up Darby, Abraham, and Bessemer, Henry, in an encyclopaedia. Write a short account of their work and explain how Darby's furnace and Bessemer's 'converter' worked. Draw diagrams to illustrate the two processes.

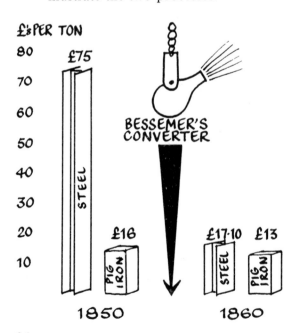

£s PER TON

BESSEMER'S CONVERTER

Changes in the price of iron and steel in ten years.

34

2

CHANGES IN TRANSPORT AND COMMUNICATIONS

When industry began to develop in the eighteenth century the lack of decent transport and communications was felt at once. Roads which had been good enough when people rarely moved away from their native village or town and met most of their needs locally could no longer cope with the sudden increase in traffic. Raw materials, fuel and machinery had now to be taken to the new factories, and the finished products had to be carried all over the country. Workpeople had to be able to move rapidly and cheaply to and from the new towns and there had to be a fast, reliable postal service for business men. There were none of these things. This is what a great traveller, Arthur Young, said about one of the roads at the end of the eighteenth century.

"Of all the cursed roads that ever disgraced this kingdom, none ever equalled that from Billericay to the *King's Head* at Tilbury. It is for near 12 miles so narrow that a mouse cannot pass by any carriage: I saw a fellow creep under his waggon to assist me to lift, if possible, my chaise [a light carriage] over a hedge. The ruts are of an incredible depth . . . the trees overgrow the road so that it is totally impervious to the sun except at a few places; And to add to all these infamous circumstances I must not forget the eternally meeting with chalk waggons: themselves frequently stuck fast, till a collection of them are in the same situation, and twenty or thirty horses may be tacked on to each, to draw them out one by one . . . "

As this was one of the main roads leading into London, you can imagine what the side roads were like.

Wherever possible heavy goods such as coal were sent round the coast by ship and then up the rivers. Unfortunately, of course, very few parts of Britain are anywhere near a stream that is deep enough for boats so that transport usually had to fall back on the dreadful roads.

These were usually mere tracks, full of mud, ruts and deep holes in winter and inches deep in dust in summer. Heavy items travelled in the springless, lumbering waggons at a snail's pace, while lighter goods could be carried on packhorses. Both methods were slow, and the roads were so wild and desolate that highway robbery was very common indeed, even though the punishment for it was death. If one's goods were valuable, then there was a good chance they would be stolen en route: if they were fragile, there was an even greater chance they would be smashed by the pounding they received on the way.

The methods by which Britain overcame her transport problems in the years 1750 to 1850 gave her almost half a century's lead over the rest of the world in the race for industrialisation.

Roads

The first transport problem to be tackled was the system of roads. At the beginning of the eighteenth century these were usually nothing more than mud tracks full of deep ruts, pools of water, holes and great boulders. Under a law of Elizabeth I each parish was supposed to repair its own roads but few did anything about it.

As traffic began to increase it was obvious that something would have to be done as the tracks rapidly became impassable in winter. The government divided the 'main' roads into sections of a few miles each and rented each stretch to a company called a Turnpike Trust which promised to improve its stretch of road and keep it in good repair. In return the company was allowed to place gates at both ends of its road and charge tolls for its use. On one turnpike the following charges were made.

Horses (being ridden)	1d	
Coaches	6d	
Carts	8d	(these were harder on the road)
Waggons	12d	(their wheels broke up the road)
20 sheep	$\frac{1}{2}$d	
20 pigs	2d	
20 cows	5d	

In relation to the wages at the time this was fairly expensive as the toll on the waggon would be about a pound at today's rates.

As always in business, some of the companies were honest, some dishonest. Some worked hard to make their roads straight, level and firm while others did absolutely nothing except collect the tolls. This is what Arthur Young said about one turnpike road towards the end of the eighteenth century.

"The road [from Tetford to Oxford] . . . is all of chalk stone, of which loose ones are everywhere rolling about to lame horses. It is full of holes, and the ruts are very deep; and withal so narrow that I

SLOW

SMALL LOADS

STOP

DANGER   MANY BREAKAGES   WINTER MUD

SHALLOW RIVERS

WHAT EXISTED

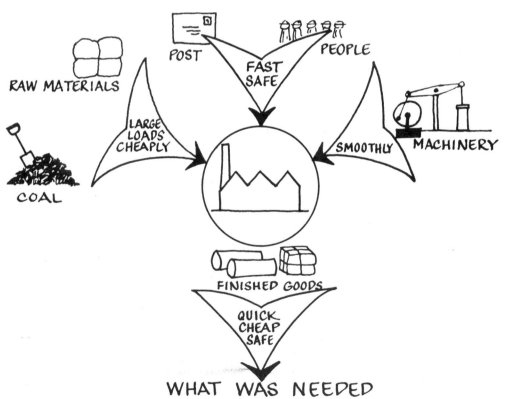

RAW MATERIALS

POST   FAST SAFE   PEOPLE

COAL   LARGE LOADS CHEAPLY   SMOOTHLY   MACHINERY

FINISHED GOODS

QUICK CHEAP SAFE

WHAT WAS NEEDED

THE RISE AND FALL OF THE ROADS IN THE INDUSTRIAL REVOLUTION

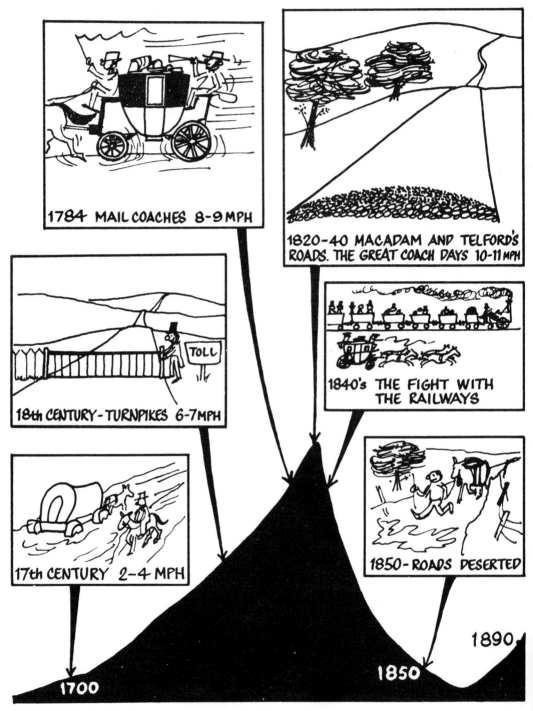

1784 MAIL COACHES 8-9 MPH

1820-40 MACADAM AND TELFORD'S ROADS. THE GREAT COACH DAYS 10-11 MPH

18th CENTURY - TURNPIKES 6-7 MPH

1840's THE FIGHT WITH THE RAILWAYS

17th CENTURY 2-4 MPH

1850 - ROADS DESERTED

1700

1850

1890

The fastest travel available.

with great difficulty got my chaise out of the way of the Witney waggons. The tolls are very dear and vilely unreasonable . . . "

Nevertheless, on the 20,000 miles of turnpike road there was a steady improvement, though the 100,000 miles of side roads became rapidly worse than ever because of the increase in traffic.

These turnpikes at their best had a gravel surface rather like some modern farm roads or private drives. Although they would seem very poor to us today they were a vast improvement on the previous tracks and they encouraged better coaches. As the worst of the bumps and holes were levelled out the coaches could be made lighter and less clumsy and consequently, faster. Some even had steel or leather springing to add to their comfort. By 1760 a fast coach could reach Ipswich from London (70 miles) in 10 hours, and Leeds (200 miles) in $2\frac{1}{2}$ days. But the cost of this kind of express travel was high: the Ipswich coach charged 1p a mile, plus tips to the driver and guard, and meals. On the Leeds trip there would be two overnight stops to be paid for as well. At present rates the single journey from London to Ipswich would work out at £15–£20: in 1967 the rail fare for the same journey was £1.

As the industrial revolution really got under way in the first thirty years of the nineteenth century road development went ahead rapidly, largely through the efforts of the two great engineers Thomas Telford and John Macadam. Both of these men realised that if the highways were to stand up to the heavy traffic it was no use placing the gravel directly on the soil. Roads, like houses, they said, must have foundations.

Telford used a layer of stone blocks on the bottom, then a 15 centimetre

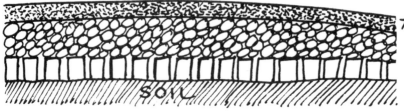

$7\frac{1}{2}$ cm RAMMED GRAVE
15 cm LARGE STONES
STONE BLOCKS

Telford's road construction—very good, but very expensive.

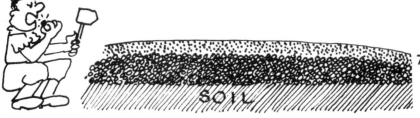

$7\frac{1}{2}$ cm VERY FINE STON
30 cm LAYER OF
$2\frac{1}{2}$ cm STONES

Macadam's road construction—good and very cheap. The bottom layer of stones had to be about $2\frac{1}{2}$ cm in diameter. The test the stone breakers used was to see if the stone would go in their mouths. If it would not, it was too large.

layer of large stones and topped this off with $7\frac{1}{2}$ centimetres of rammed gravel. Macadam believed that if the foundations were kept dry the expensive stone block base was unnecessary. His roads were made with a 30 centimetre layer of small stones finished off with $7\frac{1}{2}$ centimetres of very fine stone well rammed down. There was, of course, no tar available at the beginning of the century, but when it was introduced, the top layer of gravel was bound together with it as it is today. In honour of John Macadam this mixture of tar and gravel was called tarmacadam, or as we say today, tarmac.

As the network of better main roads spread, so coaching speeds increased. In 1811 the Holyhead coach rumbled from London to Chester in 28 hours—an average speed of 6 miles an hour. Stops for meals, to pay tolls and to change horses were included in this. Twenty years later the same journey took only 17 hours, an average speed of 10 miles an hour.

To keep up this speed horses had to be changed every few miles, but even this was such a strain that an animal on one of the main coaching routes lasted only three or four years in first class service. It was estimated that the number of horses needed by a coach for any journey was equal to the number of miles. The 200 mile journey from London to Exeter would need 200 horses in both directions!

Each coach carried fifteen passengers—four inside and eleven outside. Some of the 'outsides' sat beside the driver, some beside the guard, some on the roof and some in the luggage basket at the rear.

In the late 1830s hundreds of coaches galloped over the main turnpikes every day. Five years later they had almost vanished. The railways, offering a much faster, much cheaper and more comfortable service had arrived. For a few years there was bitter rivalry and savage quarrels between the horse men and the rail men. The coach drivers were delighted at the very frequent train accidents while the engine drivers jeered at the slowness of the coaches.

But the end was inevitable and by 1850 the roads were deserted apart from a few farm carts and private carriages, which were probably on their way to the nearest railway station. Weeds and grass began to grow across the gravel surface, and holes and ruts appeared. Although steam carriages for the road were made they were never a success because in 1861 the government passed a law which said that every mechanical vehicle on the road must have three drivers, must not go faster than 4 m.p.h. and must have a man walking in front with a red flag to warn other road users.

In 1878 the main roads were placed under the care of the county councils and gradually began to improve. In the 1880s bicycles, and in the 1890s the first snorting cars appeared, but although the Red Flag act was repealed in 1896 there were only 1,500 cars in Britain by the end of the century.

It was well into the twentieth century before tarred roads became general throughout the country and though our system of highways would seem a miracle to a man from the mid-nineteenth century, they seem to us completely inadequate for the 11,000,000 cars that jam them.

Canals

Why canals were necessary for the industrial revolution

1 MAN + 1 PACK HORSE = 3-4 CWTS

1 MAN + 1 HORSE + 1 CART = 1-2 TONS
ON VERY GOOD ROADS

1 MAN + 1 HORSE + 1 BARGE = 50-100 TONS

Although there were some turnpikes at the beginning of the Industrial Revolution, neither the roads nor the vehicles were really suitable. At their best the roads were too bumpy for fragile goods and too slow for bulky ones like coal, and the carts just could not carry heavy pieces of machinery or ironwork. The only solution seemed to be to send the material by water transport. Unfortunately, the factories, the coalmines, the quarries and the furnaces were rarely situated near the sea or a navigable river.

When the Duke of Bridgewater was faced with the problem of getting the coal from his colliery at Worsley to Manchester a few miles away, he decided that if Nature had not provided a stream, he would do so himself. He employed a brilliant engineer named James Brindley and in 1761 the first really serious canal was opened. It was an immediate success and the cost of transporting the coal from the mine to Manchester dropped by 75%. From his venture the duke is supposed to have made a profit of £100,000 a year, which was an immense sum in the eighteenth century.

At once the idea caught on for barges could not only carry very heavy loads cheaply but also ran so smoothly that fragile goods were rarely broken. For the next seventy years a network of inland waterways was dug across Britain wherever the land made it possible. Huge gangs of labourers, many of them Irish, moved from place to place excavating the great ditches and even tunnelling through mountains when necessary. These men who were known as inland navigators (later shortened to 'navigators' and then to 'navvies') were well paid and often terrorised the sleepy villages near which they happened to be working. This account of what happened in Lincolnshire in 1812 is quite typical.

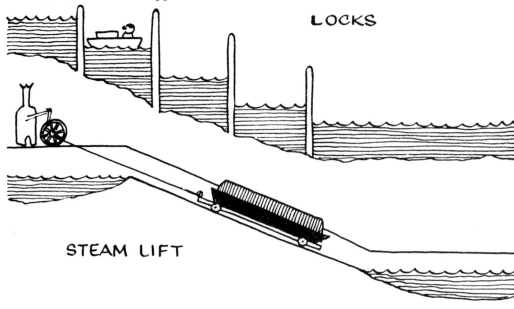

LOCKS

STEAM LIFT

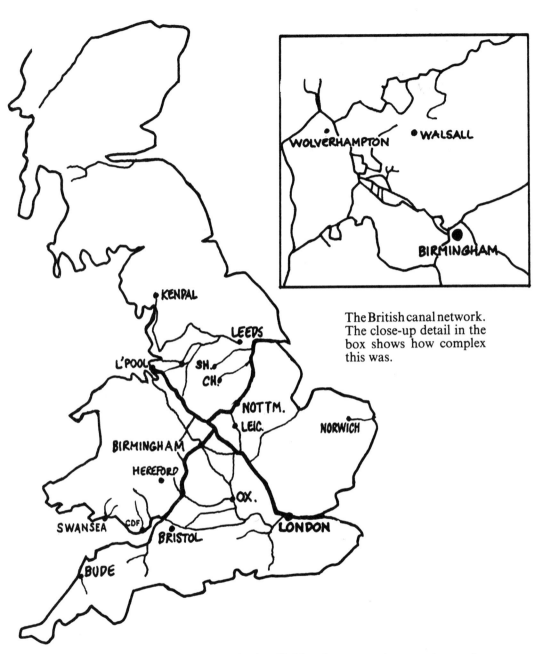

The British canal network. The close-up detail in the box shows how complex this was.

"A dispute arose on a particular Friday between the navvies and a baker named Edmonds, from Wragby, who supplied them with bread; the riot began on the west side of the river, at a public house with the sign of 'The Plough'—they drove the landlord away from his house,

43

took out his barrels, and drank the beer; having taken his sign down, they also took the baker's basket and bread, and, crossing the river, proceeded up to the village of Bardney . . . They pelted the baker with his bread, and hung his basket on the top of a tree in the village; then they attacked the *Bottle and Glass* public house—fetched barrels of beer out of the house, knocked the ends out and drank the ale; Mr Benson, a person who was then landlord of the *Angel Inn,* to prevent them entering his premises, brought or rolled out his barrels of beer himself, and by this means saved himself and his house."

One weakness of canals is that they must keep to fairly level ground. They can be taken up gentle slopes by building very expensive locks or lifts but this slows down the speed of the barges enormously. Where it was essential this was done—on the canal which connects the Thames with the Bristol Avon, for example, there are thirty locks in a mile to take the water up the side of a hill. Sometimes the canals were taken through tunnels to cross a range of hills and when this happened the bargees had to lie on their backs on the top of the boat and propel their craft through by pushing with their feet against the ceiling.

Between 1760 and 1840 almost 4,000 miles of canal were dug in Britain, and it was possible to travel by inland waters from Portsmouth to Preston in Lancashire or from Tiverton in Devon to York without once putting foot on land. If one wanted to take a round trip, one could sail on a barge from London, through Leicester, Nottingham, Leeds, Liverpool, Birmingham, Bristol and then back across England to London again.

When the railways arrived in the early 1840s the canals, like the coaches, began a bitter battle for trade. But unlike the coaches, the canals did not give up so easily. The railway companies bought up about one third of the canals to prevent competition, and traffic on most of the others dwindled as the century went on. Even so, the canals are by no means dead: of the 4,000 miles that existed in 1830 about 2,400 miles are still in use. The busiest of these carry twenty five million tons of goods a year between them, while the remainder are used for pleasure boating and floating holidays.

Railways

Much of the success of the industrial revolution was due to the improvement in the transport system of the country. Roads, canals and steamships all play their parts, but far more important was the railway.

In the eighteenth century, when heavier loads of stone and coal were being carried, the problem of cart wheels sinking into the soft muddy roads became acute. In winter the deep ruts often made the highways impassable even though the waggons were sometimes fitted with wheels two or three feet wide. All that this did was to make bigger and more dangerous ruts. It was soon obvious that the only answer was to lay down planks of wood for the cart to run along, and to prevent the timber wearing out too quickly it was covered with sheets of iron. To stop the cart wheels from slipping from this narrow track, one, or sometimes both, edges of the iron plate were turned up. As this shallow trough tended to fill up with stones and rubbish the turned-up edge was later put on the wheel itself, as it is in railway carriages today.

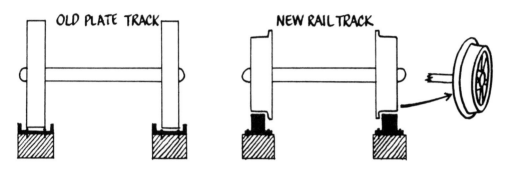

OLD PLATE TRACK   NEW RAIL TRACK

From about 1730 onwards short stretches of these 'rail roads' each a few miles long were being built all over the country, especially from quarries and coal mines to the nearest river, canal or sea port. A single horse could pull about 2 tons along them in all weathers, whereas on the ordinary roads it could usually manage no more than one ton in good conditions, and none at all in the winter.

When James Watt's steam engine appeared in 1760 engineers soon realised that here was something much better and much stronger than a horse for pulling loads, but the early machines were much too heavy and clumsy to fit into carts or carriages. The best that could be done was to place engines fitted with huge winding drums along the side of the rail-road, about a mile apart. One end of a long rope was fastened to a string of trucks and the other end to the drum, which then began to turn, pulling the waggons along. When they reached the first steam engine, they were uncoupled from the rope and fastened to one which pulled them on to the next engine.

This was a very clumsy system, and inventors began to look for ways of making a steam engine small enough and powerful enough to fit inside one of the waggons. By 1814 a number of these 'locomotives' were snorting up and down private colliery lines pulling strings of trucks. Among the more successful of these were *Puffing Billy* made by Thomas Hedley, and *Blucher,* the first locomotive to be made by the more famous George Stephenson.

These colliery lines were, of course, completely private, and were used only for carrying coal from their owners' mines to the ports or canals. In 1825, however, came the next big step towards a railway system—a public line on which anyone who wished could have his coal, beer barrels, pig iron or anything else carried for a fee. This ran from Stockton to Darlington, a distance of 11 miles, and its engineer was the famous George Stephenson. On September 27th the first real goods railway in the world opened with *Locomotion No. 1* pulling six waggons of coal, one waggon with the owners of the line, six more waggons with seats for visitors and finally, fourteen waggons for the workmen who had built the track.

Although the first train along the line pulled passengers, this idea was discounted as the speed (almost 12 miles an hour at times) was thought to be too dangerous for human beings. Goods were taken to and fro by steam locomotives but passengers travelled more respectably and more safely along the same railway lines in horse-drawn carriages.

Because of the success of the Stockton railway, it was decided to build another track, this time from Manchester to Liverpool. Once again the engineer was George Stephenson, and although the line was intended mainly for goods, the owners decided that they would carry passengers if anyone cared to risk his life.

When the line was ready the owners could not make up their minds whether to haul the trucks with stationary engines and long ropes or with locomotives. To settle the issue they announced a competition with a prize of £500 for the best engine. Four locomotives were entered for the trials—the *Sanspareil*, the *Novelty*, the *Perseverance* and, of course, *The Rocket* built by George Stephenson and his son, Robert. This is how John Dixon, Stephenson's assistant, wrote to his brother after the trials.

October 16th, 1829.

"Dear James,

We have finished the grand experiments on the Engines and G.S. and R.S. [the Stephensons, that is] has come off triumphant and of course will take hold of the £500. . . . The Rocket is the best Engine I have ever seen. . . .

The Sanspareil *burns nearly double the quantity of coke that* The Rocket *does and mumbles and roars and rolls about like an Empty Beer Butt on a rough Pavement. . . . She is very ugly and the Boiler runs out. . . .*

The . . . Novelty *seemed to dart away like a Greyhound for a bit but every trial he had some mishap, first an explosion of gas which Burst his Bellows then his feed pipe blew up and finally some internal joint of this hidden flue thro his boiler. . . .*

46

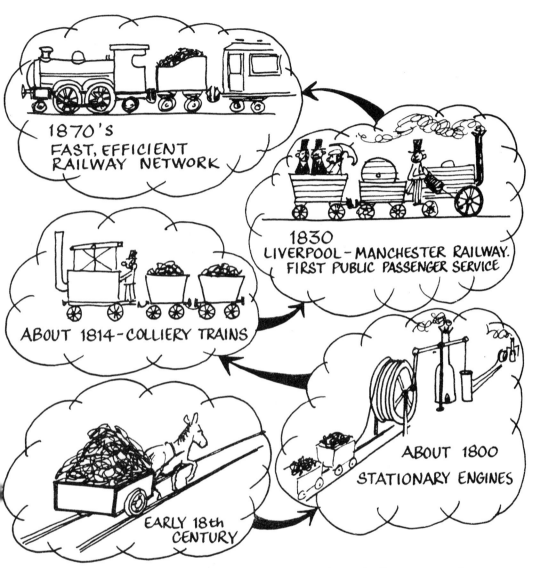

1870's
FAST, EFFICIENT
RAILWAY NETWORK

1830
LIVERPOOL – MANCHESTER RAILWAY.
FIRST PUBLIC PASSENGER SERVICE

ABOUT 1814 - COLLIERY TRAINS

ABOUT 1800
STATIONARY ENGINES

EARLY 18th
CENTURY

Burstall [the Perseverance] . . . *was the last of all to start and a sorrowful start it was; full 6 miles an hour cranking away like an old Wickerwork pair of Panniers on a Cantering Cuddy Ass. . . . "*

In 1830 the regular train service began. To the amazement of the owners there were far more passengers than they could manage so that they carried goods only when they could find a spare engine. The new form of transport sent the country wild: everyone wanted railways, and hundreds of small companies began to build short lengths of line from one town to the next.

All through the 1840s and 50s the railway madness swept the country. Lines crept outwards in all directions, joined up with one another and filled the country with a network. Tens of thousands of navvies who in the earlier part of the century had built the canals now dug cuttings, built embankments, tunnelled through mountains, threw up bridges and stations and laid down track.

The railway catered for three classes of passenger. The rich travelled in first class carriages which were almost identical with stage coaches, with padded seats and glass windows; the middle class travelled in second class carriages, which normally had hard wooden seats, a roof but no sides; and the poor travelled in open trucks like coal waggons, often without even benches to sit on. In 1844, however, Parliament ordered that every passenger must be given some covering from the weather and that at least one train every day must run along every track charging one 'penny' a mile.

As the century went on railway travel became faster, more comfortable and, most important of all, safer, for the early trains were death traps. In 1875, for example, brakes were still not fitted except to the engine itself, and tests that year showed that a 14 carriage train travelling at 47 miles an hour took $\frac{3}{4}$ mile to stop after the brakes had been applied. Brakes were not made compulsory on all coaches until 1889. Signals were introduced gradually to replace the railway policemen who indicated whether the line was clear or not by waving their truncheons or flags.

There was no heating in the early trains except iron hot water bottles which could be hired at stations. Wealthy passengers often hired two— one to sit on, the other for their feet. Steam heated pipes were first used in 1892, the same year in which the first trains with corridors ran from Paddington. Dining carriages had been introduced a few years earlier, and these two between them did much to avoid the mad stampede along the platform to the buffet and lavatories which took place every time a long-distance train stopped at a station.

In the last years of the century trains were reaching speeds of well over 70 miles an hour on short stretches and averaging over 50 miles an hour on long journeys. The 200 mile trip from London to Exeter, for example, took only twenty minutes longer seventy-five years ago than it does today.

1830	20 MILES OF TRACK
1840	850 MILES
1860	10,400 MILES
1880	18,000 MILES
1896	22,000 MILES

How the railways grew in England

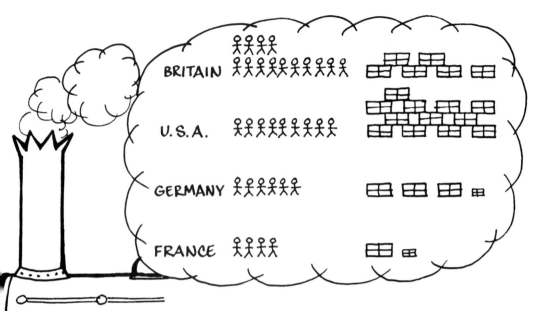

Railway figures for 1886. Each figure represents half a million passengers: each large parcel represents half a million tons of goods. The large American tonnage of goods is mainly wheat. Because Britain is smaller than any of the other three countries, she had fewer miles of railway track, but her lines were by far the busiest in the world.

1. Why was it necessary to provide a better road system in the nineteenth century?
2. (a) What were the advantages of canals over roads? (b) What were the disadvantages?
3. How does a lock work? Without looking at the illustration draw a simple diagram to illustrate your explanation.
4. What were the turnpike roads and why were they so unpopular?
5. In history books and encyclopaedias look up *one* of the following and write a short account of his life and work:
   (a) Thomas Telford, (b) John Macadam.
6. Explain some of the problems connected with coach travel in the early part of the nineteenth century. What eventually caused the disappearance of the coach as a means of transport?
7. (a) Imagine yourself to have been a passenger on one of the first trains. Write a short account of your journey explaining how you felt.
   (b) Imagine yourself to have been a passenger 50 years later. What changes would you have noticed?
8. Explain the ways in which the railways became a boon in nineteenth century Britain.

3

PEOPLE AT WORK

Early traditional working conditions

If you could visit a factory as it was in the first forty years of the nineteenth century your first impression would be that you had arrived at a prison. Its walls would be tall and grim and its windows small and often barred with iron. Once inside, however, you would realise that it was not a gaol, for many convicts received better treatment than the factory workers.

Perhaps the first thing that you would notice would be the dreadful conditions in which the people worked. To help stop the cotton threads from snapping, the inside of the textile factories was kept very hot and very moist, the temperature usually being between 26 and 29 degrees. This noisy, steamy atmosphere was thick with dust and fluff from the cotton fibres, and over all hung the unpleasant smell from the open lavatory buckets at one end of the room. It is not surprising that the death rate from tuberculosis and lung diseases among the people who had to work for up to eighteen hours a day in such conditions was horrifying.

Although the working day was so long, no one, not even small children, was allowed to sit down except during the lunch interval. Even during the short breakfast and tea breaks many factories kept their engines running so that the workers had to eat with one hand and operate their looms or jennies with the other. These long hours spent hunched over the machines added stomach complaints, varicose veins and ulcers to the long list of diseases from which the workers suffered. Perhaps even worse, small children, who often had to bend their bodies into unnatural positions to do their jobs properly, frequently grew up with twisted spines, crooked thighs and knock-knees.

Finally, as if natural diseases did not do enough in the way of killing and maiming, there were always the machines themselves waiting to mangle workers who became caught in them. There were no laws to compel factory owners to cover belts, wheels and moving parts, so that these were left completely unguarded. At the end of a twelve or fourteen hour day it was all too easy for a weary adult, let alone a child, to make a mistake and get caught in the machinery. In 1833, of every five accident cases received at Manchester Infirmary, two were the result of factory machines.

Perhaps the next thing that would surprise you in your factory visit would be the number of children employed. At the beginning of the century there were no laws at all about the age at which boys and girls could start work, nor the length of their working day. Although some factories took them at five, it was more usual to start at the age of seven when they were more able to stay awake for the ten, twelve or fourteen hours that were expected of them.

Of course, poor children had always worked throughout history, but until the industrial revolution their tasks had usually been outdoor jobs such as weeding, bird-scaring and looking after animals. These may have been monotonous, but they were reasonably healthy, not very hard, and there was always an opportunity to relax. Now, in the factories everyone was tied to the pace of the steam engine and as long as this kept pounding, no one dared stop.

There had been machines before the nineteenth century, but on the whole they were fairly clumsy and needed the power of a water mill, a horse, or at least an adult to drive them. Even such simple machinery as the loom or the spinning jenny, both of which were used in the home, needed the strength of a man, but with the arrival of steam power all of this changed. The engine now provided the energy, and women and children could pull the levers to operate the equipment as easily as a man, and far more cheaply.

From a factory owner's point of view this was a wonderful situation for it meant that he could now employ women and children instead of men, and so save himself large sums in wages. Instead of having to pay 75p or 80p a week for each male worker, he could now get three or four workers for the same price, as women received only about 35p a week and children 17p. An additional benefit for some employers was that the women and children could be bullied and ill-treated more easily than men. So it was that husbands often had to remain at home, unemployed, while their wives and children worked in the mill to support the family. At other times factory owners would refuse to employ a man unless he would agree to bring his wife and a number of children as well.

The early years of the Industrial Revolution were a cruel time in any big manufacturing city. The harshness and greed of many of the factory owners were passed on by the foremen to the workers under them, often because the men in charge were themselves threatened with dismissal if they did not collect enough in fines or get an almost impossible amount of work done. Sometimes the overlookers seemed to delight in inflicting savage punishments on the women and children, and slave dealers from the West Indies were genuinely horrified when they saw the conditions of cruelty which existed in the textile mills.

While the floggings and beatings were bad enough, it was the injustice of the harsh fines that hurt the adult workers most of all. When a man's

52

How many factory owners exploited the workers.

A woman and two children would often cost less than one man in wages and still do the same work.

Workers often paid all or part of their wages in tokens which could be spent at the owner's shop. Goods were of poorer quality and cost more here—the profits went to the factory owner.

Workers were often compelled to live in the factory houses which were cheaply built hovels let at far too high a rent—the profit to the factory owner, of course.

wage was 75p a week and woman's half of that, he could not afford to lose any of it in fines, particularly if they were unreasonable. Here is a set of rules which were typical of those pinned up in many workshops and mills in the north.

1. "Doors will be closed 10 minutes after the engine starts and no weaver will be admitted until breakfast time. Any weaver absent will be fined 3d for each loom." [As a weaver normally was in charge of two looms this meant a fine of '6d', or half a day's pay for a woman.]

2. "Weavers leaving the room without the consent of the overseer while the engine is working, fine 3d." [This included going to the lavatory or getting a drink.]

3. "Weavers not providing themselves with nippers or shears will be fined 1d a day." [That is, they had to provide their own tools.]

4. "All shuttles, wheels, brushes, oilcans, windows, etc, found broken will be paid for by the weaver."

5. "If any hand in the mill be seen talking to another, whistling or singing, he will be fined 6d."

6. "Any hand opening a window will be fined 1/–" [can you think why?]

One Lancashire mill fined workers 5 pence if they came to the factory dirty, and another 5 pence if they went to wash. In another any worker who was ill and failed to find someone else to do his job was fined 30 pence: at today's rates this would be over £6.

Some unscrupulous employers went even further. They actually advanced the factory clocks by 15 minutes in the morning so that all of the workers were late and were fined. By evening the clock would somehow lose half an hour so that it was 15 minutes slow—and the owner would get a quarter of an hour's work from his men without payment. In other factories there were two clocks, one a normal one, and the other driven by the steam engine. If the engine was running slowly, then the clock ran slowly so that the employees might have to work an extra hour or more. If the engine was running quickly, then the factory closed at the time by the ordinary clock.

Although they were a very small minority, there were some employers who genuinely tried to do what they thought best for their work-people. But even these 'good' factory owners did not seem to realise two of the worst cruelties of the system—the incredibly long hours and the employment of children. Twelve to fourteen hours a day from Monday to Saturday with a 'short' day of four hours to clean the machinery on Sunday was quite usual, even for small children. If you look at the chart below you will see that the factory worker of 1820 put in as many hours in a week as his modern counterpart does in a fortnight—and the nineteenth century man had no holidays except Good Friday and Christmas Day.

The evils and cruelties of the factories fell on everyone who worked

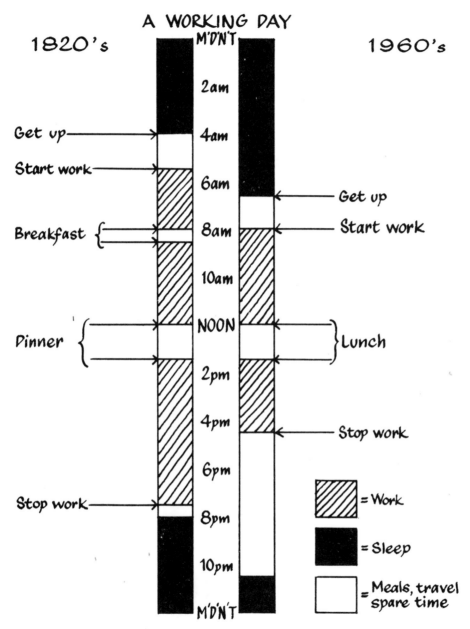

A WORKING DAY

1820's

1960's

M'D'N'T

2am

4am — Get up

6am

8am — Breakfast {

10am

NOON

Dinner {

2pm

4pm

6pm

8pm — Stop work

10pm

M'D'N'T

Get up

Start work

Lunch

Stop work

= Work

= Sleep

= Meals, travel spare time

in them, men, women and children alike, but on one group they fell far more savagely than anyone else. These were the parish apprentices. They were children whose parents were either dead or had abandoned them so that they had to be brought up in the work-house. To get some idea of how these poor creatures lived you have only to read *Oliver Twist*,

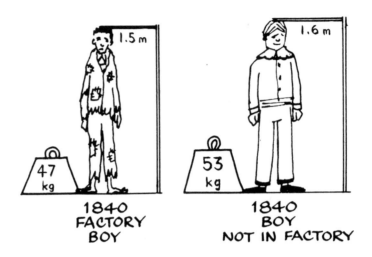

1.5 m

47 kg

1.6 m

53 kg

1840 FACTORY BOY

1840 BOY NOT IN FACTORY

but to avoid even the small expense of a work-house upbringing many towns, especially London, sent their orphans to the manufacturing cities of the midlands and north to become 'apprentices'. This really meant that the children were forced to work in a factory from the age of about seven until they were twenty-one without any wages at all. They were supposed to be provided with food, clothing and shelter but in the interests of profit they were usually given only enough to keep them alive, and they worked until they dropped. This is what John Fielden said about parish apprentices in 1836.

" . . . The most heart-rending cruelties were practised upon these unoffending and friendless creatures who were thus consigned to the charge of the master manufacturers: they were harassed to the brink of death by excess labour, they were flogged, fettered and tortured . . . they were in many cases starved to the bone while flogged at their work. . . . "

They lived in barracks near the mill and were often organised in two shifts. One group worked twelve hours during the day and the other worked twelve at night, and as one group got up, the other crawled under the same filthy blankets.

The punishments inflicted on these defenceless children are almost unbelievable. For the smallest mistakes they had heavy iron weights hung round their necks as they worked or had iron vices screwed to their ears. One boy from a midlands nail-making factory told a government official that the usual punishment there was to drive a nail through the offender's ear into the wooden bench.

As industry grew bigger and bigger so the coal mines had to go

56

deeper and deeper to meet the steam engines' unceasing call for fuel. And bad though conditions were in the factories, they were worse in the pits. The hours were as long, the air was as foul, the pay was as low, but in addition there was the danger, the darkness, the water and above all the terrible physically hard work.

As in the factories, the owners were completely unscrupulous and thought only of their profits. There was little attempt at safety measures and terrible accidents through breaking ladders and ropes were everyday occurrences. Miners were paid by the tub, and if a 4¼ hundredweight tub was not quite full, the owners paid nothing at all and got, say, 3¾ hundredweights free. If the tub was over full, the miner got nothing extra. If there happened to be some slack among the coal, which was sometimes unavoidable, not only did the unfortunate worker receive nothing at all for that tub, but he was fined into the bargain. Frequently a man worked the whole week and found when he went to the foreman for his wages that he actually owed the master money as his fines totalled more than his wages.

Men, women and children toiled side by side in the damp darkness of the pits, and surprising as it may seem, children usually began to work underground at an earlier age than they did in the factories. The youngest children (4–6 year-olds) were usually trappers. This is what the government report of 1842 says of their job:

"The ventilation [of the mine] again depends entirely on the trap-doors being kept shut and on their being properly closed after the carriages conveying the coal have passed them.

TRAPPING   DRAWING

The youngest children in the mines are entrusted with this important office. Their duty consists in sitting in a little hole, scooped out for them in the side of the gates behind each door, where they sit with a string in their hands attached to the door, and pull it the moment they hear the corves [the carriages for conveying the coal] . . . they are in the pit the whole time it is worked, frequently about 12 hours a day. They sit, moreover, in the dark, often with a damp floor to stand on. . . . "

At six or seven they moved on either to carrying the coal in baskets or pulling trucks along the low galleries, harnessed to the wagon like animals. This is what the report said of one girl:

"Margaret Leveston, 6 years old . . . been down at coal-carrying six weeks; makes ten to fourteen journeys a day; carries full 56 lb. of coal in a wooden backit [basket]. . . . "

Just imagine a 6 year-old carrying half-a-hundredweight of coal all day long.

Another girl, Ellison Jack, 11 years old, carried a basket containing 1-1½ hundredweights of coal all day long, 84 feet from the pit face, then up an eighteen-foot ladder, along another tunnel about 4 feet high to a second 18-foot ladder, along a third tunnel, up a third ladder, along a fourth ladder to the tub. Her task was to fill four or five tubs, each holding almost a quarter of a ton, every day. The report adds that the baskets of coal this eleven-year-old girl had to carry often took two people to hoist them on to her back.

Because of the water, the filth and the heat, men, women and children often worked stark naked in the slushy, black mud in the dark tunnels. It is little wonder that they lived like animals below ground, and often little better when they reached the surface.

Working twelve or more hours under the ground, and going down before dawn and coming up after dark, many literally saw daylight only on Sunday. It is little wonder, too, that until well into the nineteenth century a condemned criminal in Scotland would be offered the choice of execution—or going into the coal mines.

Finally, a word about the chimney sweeps who are perhaps the best-known of all the unfortunate children of the industrial revolution. Most of these were parish children but some were from private homes. To a starving family a good offer from a master sweep for a specially small four- or five-year-old must have been very tempting.

These pitiful apprentices climbed the narrow, twisting chimneys not only to clean them, but also to put out fires, and more often than not they slept on bags of soot. Rarely washed, brutally treated and in constant

Chimneys of wood-burning fires were wide and straight, often with iron rungs for sweeping.

Chimneys of coal-burning fires had to be narrow. In towns they often had twists and bends.

Some chimneys were only 23 cm square, and yet these were swept by climbing boys. To get some idea of just what this meant, take a sheet or card and in the centre cut out a square 23 cm by 23 cm, and then try to get through it. Most probably not even your head will pass through—yet just over a hundred years ago boys, and girls, were crawling along tunnels of this size, sweeping as they went.

danger of being trapped or suffocated in the winding tunnels, they cannot have looked forward very much to living. Perhaps mercifully, the soot frequently caused cancers and many died at a very early age.

Although all too many masters behaved with appalling cruelty and greed towards their workpeople there were a few far-sighted men who realised that the working class were not a different race of human beings and that perhaps more could be done if they were treated with humanity. Some were wealthy noblemen like Lord Shaftsbury, while others were men of humble birth who had made fortunes, like Robert Owen. Owen, in particular, tried methods long ahead of his time. He built good houses for the workers in his huge cotton mills, started schools for the children instead of making them work, provided shops where his workpeople could buy goods cheaply, organised entertainments for them and reduced their hours to, by the ideas of the time, an outrageous degree.

It was men like these who showed the way, compelling the government to make enquiries into the way industry and mines were being run (see page 57) and causing conditions to improve gradually. The workers themselves played their part by forming trade unions which, although weak and not very effective at first, gradually grew to be a great power, as we shall see. By the end of the century, although there were still many things wrong in the factories and many injustices, the worst of the horrors of the industrial revolution were just a memory in the minds of the few factory men and women who had lived to old age.

The rise of trade unions

When you read about the appalling conditions and low wages in the factories and mines you may well wonder why the working people did not do anything about it. Today, of course, if employees feel that they are not being paid enough or that there is something wrong with their conditions of work, they can usually get matters put right by asking their trade union to discuss the situation with the employers. If this fails, the union may call a strike of its members and even ask other unions to stop work to force the employer to give way. At the beginning of the nineteenth century, the few unions that existed were small and had little power. The wealthy employers were in complete control.

Before the industrial revolution most people worked in their own homes or in very small groups so that there was little opportunity for them to discuss wages and conditions. As the factory system began to grow in the eighteenth century the workers came together and formed small trade unions to fight for better wages and conditions. The employers hated this as they thought that better wages for the workers would mean less profit for themselves.

After the French Revolution, which was a rising in which the poor overthrew the rich, the government was afraid that the union meetings were being used to plot rebellion. They passed a series of laws in 1799 called the Combination Acts, which made it illegal for more than six people to meet to discuss conditions of work.

In the next twenty-five years thousands of workers were prosecuted under these Acts, but even so some of the trade unions managed to survive by meeting in secret. Often the members were in disguise so that spies could not tell who they were. Because of the danger of being betrayed, new members were often led blindfolded to meetings and swore an oath on the Bible or a human skull that if they revealed the

60

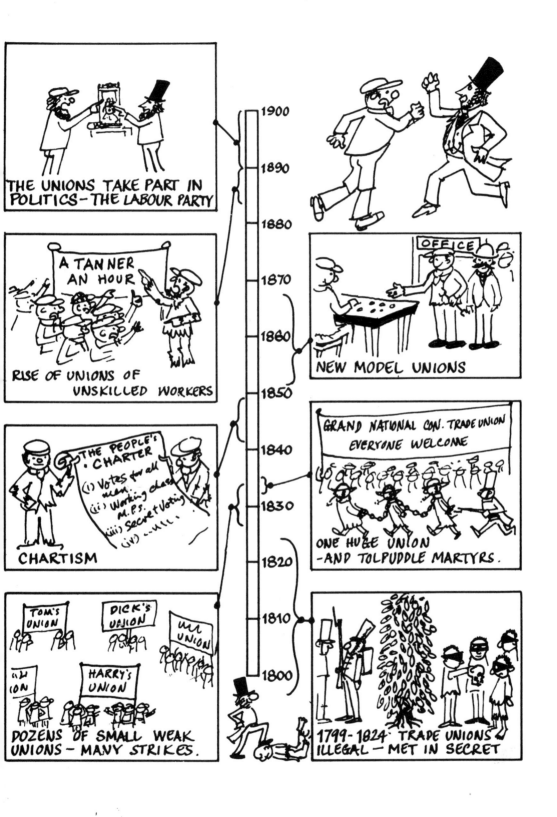

secrets they should be killed. Other unions managed to stay alive by pretending they were clubs, but messages about work would be passed in secret when they met.

After a great struggle in Parliament the hated Combination Acts were repealed in 1824. Like children let out from an over-strict teacher's class, the unions went mad when they were given their freedom. Hundreds of small, independent unions were set up overnight—and disappeared just as quickly. Small strikes broke out everywhere, but because they were small and because there were plenty of unemployed the employers just dismissed the workers involved and took on new men. Often the secretaries of the unions collected subscriptions from their members and then disappeared with the money. Even if they were traced, there was little that could be done.

After a few years it was obvious that the small unions were powerless, and in 1834 an attempt was made to form one huge union which took in all trades. This was called the Grand National Consolidated Trade Union, but it was no more successful than the small ones because what suited, say, the carpenters, did not suit the engineers, what was an advantage to the spinners might be a disadvantage to the weavers. What finally killed the monster union, however, despite the million members it claimed to have, was the case of Tolpuddle labourers.

In this small, backward village in Dorset five farm workers tried to join a branch of the Grand National. As part of the ceremony they had to be blindfolded and with their hands on a painting of a skull they repeated an oath of secrecy about the society.

Because the Combination Acts no longer were in force the men could not be prosecuted for joining a trade union, but the magistrates managed to find an old law which said that it was illegal for men to take oaths in the way the Tolpuddle labourers had done. For having repeated in all honesty those few words, the five men were sentenced to be transported to Tasmania as convicts for seven years. After this savage attack most workers were afraid of joining trade unions and interest in them died down.

In the 1840s the workers tried a new approach. They tried to persuade Parliament to change the laws so that the ordinary man could have some say in the way the country and industry was run. Great meetings were held up and down the country for what was called 'The People's Charter'. These Chartists, as they were called, asked for six things:

1. There should be a new parliament every year.
2. All adult men should be allowed to vote.
3. Members of Parliament should be paid.
4. Each constituency should have the same number of voters.
5. Voting should be in secret by a ballot box.

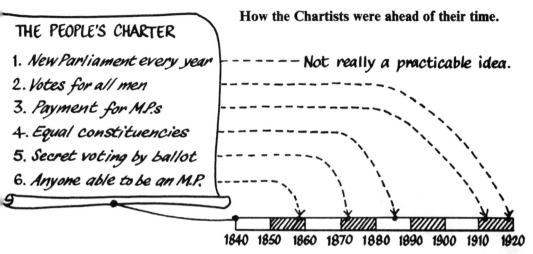

How the Chartists were ahead of their time.

THE PEOPLE'S CHARTER

1. *New Parliament every year* — — — — — — Not really a practicable idea.
2. *Votes for all men*
3. *Payment for M.P.s*
4. *Equal constituencies*
5. *Secret voting by ballot*
6. *Anyone able to be an M.P.*

1840 1850 1860 1870 1880 1890 1900 1910 1920

The dotted lines show when their demands were actually granted.

6. Anyone should be allowed to become an M.P., not only those who
    owned property.
As you see in the diagram, all of these conditions except annual parlia-
ments were finally granted, but most of them not until long after many
of the Chartists were dead.

By 1848, however, Chartism was dead, largely because the huge
petition containing three million signatures which the organisers took
to Parliament was found to be partly a forgery. It looked as if hope for
the workers had gone.

In the 1850s a new kind of union was formed among the highly
skilled men such as engineers, mechanics, shipbuilders and others who
would be difficult to replace if they went on strike. Any employer could
get another navvy or machine operator, but it would be hard to find a
man who could make or repair a steam engine if the engineers decided
to stop work. These model unions, as they were called, collected from
each member 5 pence a week, which was far more than a factory worker
or farm labourer could afford.

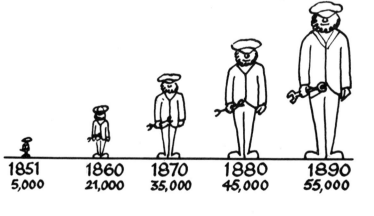

How the first of the
New Model Unions,
The Amalgamated
Society of Engineers
grew in size.
This shows how
effective it was.

1851   1860   1870   1880   1890
5,000   21,000   35,000   45,000   55,000

Estimated numbers of union and non-union workers in 1890.

	Union	Non-union
Metal workers Engineers Miners	20	80
Builders	15	85
Textiles Woodworkers	10	90
Transport	5	95
All others		Almost 100

Notice how the majority of union men were in the skilled trades while there are almost none at all among agricultural, clerical and unskilled workers, or shop assistants.

With the money the engineers were able to employ a full-time secretary to run their union rather than let one of their members do it in his spare time as was the usual practice. Also, if they went on strike the union had enough money to pay the men at least part of their wages. With these advantages it is not surprising that the unions of skilled craftsmen grew rapidly in numbers and in power, and they managed to gain great benefits for their members.

The unskilled workers such as the dockers, the labourers and the women in factories, were still unorganised and very much at the mercy of their employers, but in the 1880s these too began to fight for their rights. Surprisingly enough, one of the first important strikes on behalf of these workers was led by a woman, Mrs. Annie Besant, who organised a strike by the girls who made matches under dreadful and dangerous conditions. The 800 girls marched from their factory in the East End of London to the smart West End, where their poverty horrified the people they met. They won their wage increase. The next year (1889) a strike of the dockers, led by Tom Mann and John Burns, brought an even bigger shock to the people of London. Sympathy flared up for the ragged, ill-fed men who were paid 2p or $2\frac{1}{2}$p an hour and then only when there was work for them. The dockers, too, won their demand for a wage of 3p an hour.

How the unions grew in 76 years.

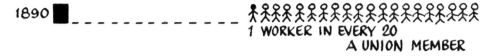

1890 — 1 WORKER IN EVERY 20 A UNION MEMBER

1964 — 8 WORKERS IN EVERY 20 UNION MEMBERS

0 1 2 3 4 5 6 7 8 9 10
MILLIONS OF MEMBERS

The position of unskilled workers was still very insecure, but at least the public had recognised that they had a right to a living wage.

In the last twenty years of the century the unions realised that fighting the employers one by one for better wages and conditions was a slow, wasteful process. It would be much better, they thought, to have members of the working class in parliament to try to get the improvements made by law. So the unions took to politics.

At first union members supported the Liberal party and in the 1880s managed to get a few M.P.s called Lib-Labs elected. But many people thought that the working class should have its own party and with this in mind a Scottish miner, Keir Hardie, founded the first Labour Party in Britain in 1888. Three years later Hardie himself, John Burns of the dockers, and J. H. Wilson, won seats in Parliament to become the first labour M.P.s. Although all three lost at the next election, the first big step had been taken and ever since the state of the Labour party has been closely tied up with the trade unions.

Industrial reforms

The conditions in the factories and mines which you read about were so unbelievably bad that it seems impossible that the government did not do anything about them the moment they arose. Unfortunately, many of the M.P.s owned either factories or slum estates and did not wish to pass any laws which might lower their incomes.

The first sign that Parliament felt it ought to do something about protecting the children at least came in 1819 when an act was passed which laid down that no one under sixteen must work more than twelve hours a day. But twelve hours is a very long time: imagine how you would feel if school lasted from 9 a.m. till 9 p.m. with only half an hour for lunch and another half hour for tea. In practice, however, the act had little effect as there was no one to see that it was obeyed. There were no police and the magistrates who were responsible for enforcing

65

the law were nearly all owners of the factories, so that the children still toiled for anything up to eighteen hours a day at busy times.

Fourteen years later a much more serious attempt to improve conditions was made in an act which said that no one under the age of nine must be employed *at all,* and that children aged 9–13 must not work more than nine hours a day and must have two hours schooling in the factory. This was a real step in the right direction because a number of inspectors were appointed to visit each factory and report on it. Unfortunately, there were far too few inspectors so that it was reckoned each factory would be visited about once in ten years. In any case, there was no way of proving how old the children were, and if the factory owner said that a 6 or 7 year-old boy was twelve, there was nothing the inspector could do.

However, the inspectors did do much good: for one thing, they reported on the terrible 'schools' which some factories set up to comply with the law. Many of the 'teachers' could neither read nor write, and one 'school' was held in the boiler room by the stoker, who gabbled a few words to his 'pupils' in between shovelling coal into the furnace.

To help the inspectors in their task the government passed a bill in 1836 which compelled every birth, death and marriage to be registered. Now, if there was an argument about a child's age, the inspector had only to check on the birth certificate.

Although conditions were still terrible in the factories a good beginning had been made. Unfortunately the regulations did not apply to all factories, and the mines, which were far worse, were completely untouched. The government then began a survey of the collieries and in 1842 a commissioners' report shocked the whole nation. You can read part of this document on pages 17 and 57. Few people outside the mining towns and villages realised that children from four upwards worked for twelve hours a day in pitch darkness, or that half-naked women and older children were harnessed to trucks like animals for a few pence a week.

Parliament acted at once and in 1842 women, girls and boys below the age of 10 were banned from working underground, though they could still work on the surface sorting the coal.

The Government was still shocked by the mines report when it passed another act for the factories two years later. This one reduced the age at which children could start work to 8, and shortened the working day of children from 8–13 to $6\frac{1}{2}$ hours. Women's hours were reduced to 12 a day, and they were given further protection by other clauses such as the one which made it compulsory to guard machines to prevent accidents to women and girls whose long clothing or hair was frequently caught in the whirling belts and wheels. Employers who broke the law were fined more heavily.

Children's shortening working day.

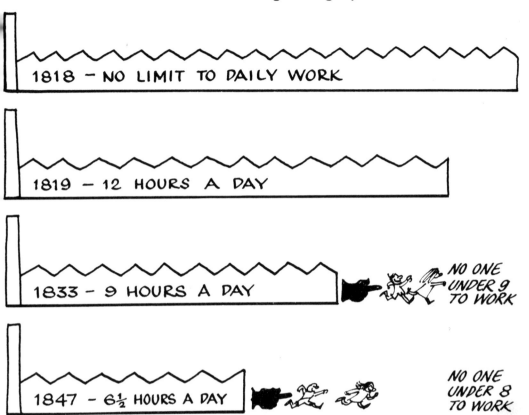

1818 — NO LIMIT TO DAILY WORK

1819 — 12 HOURS A DAY

1833 — 9 HOURS A DAY

NO ONE UNDER 9 TO WORK

1847 — 6½ HOURS A DAY

NO ONE UNDER 8 TO WORK

By this time children were reasonably well protected, though if today we had to go through what they did we should think we were being treated as slaves. The biggest sufferers in the factories were now the women who were still working far too hard. In 1847 came the last major factory act of the nineteenth century when Parliament decided that no woman must work more than ten hours a day. Although this act was apparently meant to help women, in practice the men benefited too. So many women were employed in the factories that when they finished, work came to a standstill and the men had to leave as well.

Thus by the middle of the century the major battles for better conditions in industry had been won, although there was still plenty of hardship and harshness in the factories. 9 year-old children, for example, could still be compelled to work well over 40 hours a week. In the last fifty years a number of minor acts were passed to help the workers, and the growing power of the Trade Unions did much to make the factories safer and more bearable, even if not pleasant places in which to work.

1. Explain why factory employers would prefer to use children to adults in their factories, and say also why it became easier to employ children.
2. Who were the Parish Apprentices and what was so cruel about their treatment?
3. Find out all you can about Robert Owen from history books and encyclopaedias and write a brief account of his life and work.
4. Explain briefly what you understand by the term 'Trade Union'.
5. What in your opinion are the functions of a Trade Union?
6. What caused Trade Unions to begin?
7. Find out what you can about *one* of the following from history books and encyclopaedias and write about it in as much detail as possible: (*a*) The Grand National Consolidated Trade Union, (*b*) the Combination Laws, (*c*) the Tolpuddle Martyrs, (*d*) the Chartists.
8. What do you think prevented M.P.s from reforming industrial working conditions in the early nineteenth century?
9. From this section, and from what you have gathered earlier in this book, imagine you were a child working in a factory or a mine in the early nineteenth century. Write a composition 'My Working Day', and try to describe in great detail how hard the life was. You might like to read Chapter 4 before attempting this question.

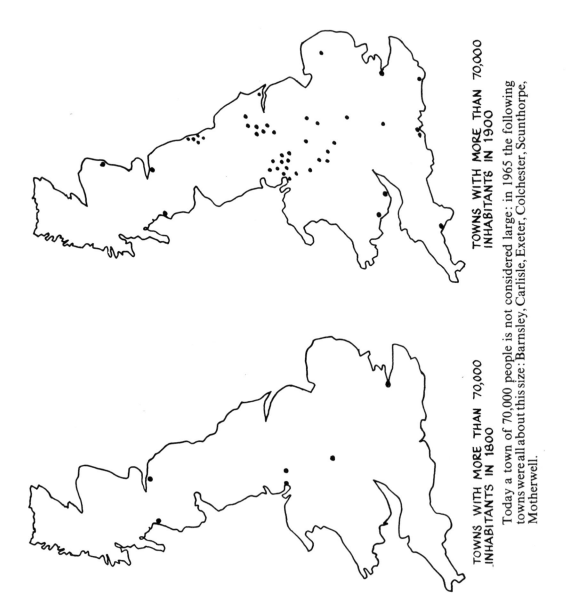

TOWNS WITH MORE THAN 70,000
INHABITANTS IN 1900

TOWNS WITH MORE THAN 70,000
INHABITANTS IN 1800

Today a town of 70,000 people is not considered large: in 1965 the following towns were all about this size: Barnsley, Carlisle, Exeter, Colchester, Scunthorpe, Motherwell.

4

TOWN LIFE

One of the most remarkable changes which took place in the nineteenth century was the rapid growth in the size of the towns, especially those in the midlands and north of England and in the industrial areas of Scotland. Many tiny villages became large towns, and small towns became huge, sprawling, overcrowded cities. This is how three typical industrial areas grew in population between 1801 and 1901.

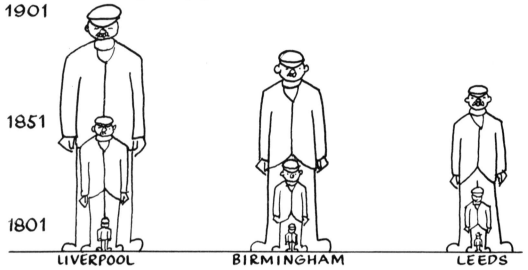

This chart shows how the proportion of town dwellers to countrymen changed during the century.

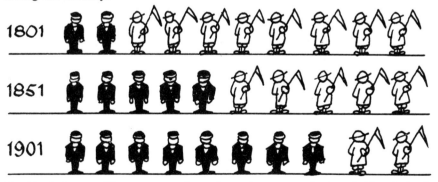

(See Book 4, page 51, to compare how these changes took place in Russia in the twentieth century).

| WILTSHIRE | 1801 | 184,000 |
| (AGRICULTURAL) | 1901 | 271,000 |

The difference in population growth between a typical agricultural county and an industrial one.

| LANCASHIRE | 1801 | 670,000 |
| (INDUSTRIAL) | 1901 | 4,400,000 |

It is easy to see how the population built up. A factory would be set up in a town and several hundred workers and their families would pour in from the nearby countryside. These new workers would need houses and shops, and the factory owner would need transport to bring in coal, raw cotton and other materials. This would mean that builders, carpenters, bricklayers, labourers, horse drivers, engineers, shopkeepers and navvies would have to move into the town. In their turn all of these newcomers would want houses, more shops, more transport and, later on, schools, hospitals, churches and entertainments. This would mean yet more builders, carpenters and labourers; more shopkeepers, cobblers, tailors and other craftsmen; more horse drivers, engineers, porters, mechanics; schoolteachers, clergymen, nurses, doctors, postmen, lawyers, innkeepers, undertakers, park-keepers and all the dozens of people who help to keep a town running.

Because many of the industrial towns grew so rapidly the houses were usually long rows of flimsy hovels jammed together as tightly as possible round the factory. One row was separated from the next by a 'court'—a strip of mud about six feet wide often with the lavatory at one end and the pump a few yards away. The lavatory was no more than a deep hole with a wooden shack above it, and like the pump often served twenty or more houses. As a result this pit soon overflowed. Some of the filth soaked into the well, but most of it ran in a sluggish, stinking stream laden with rubbish from the houses, down the centre of the court. The trickles from the different rows of houses joined up to form a disgusting river of sewage which ran either down the gutters of the main road or into a ditch at the rear of the buildings.

Here is part of a government report written in 1838. This actually refers to London, but the towns of Lancashire, Yorkshire and Nottingham were quite as bad, if not worse.

"**Virginia-row.** In the centre of this street there is a gutter into which potato parings, the refuse of vegetable and animal matter of all kinds, the dirty water from the washing of clothes and of the houses are all poured, and where they stagnate and putrefy. . . . From Virginia-row to Shoreditch, a mile in extent, all the lanes, courts and alleys in the

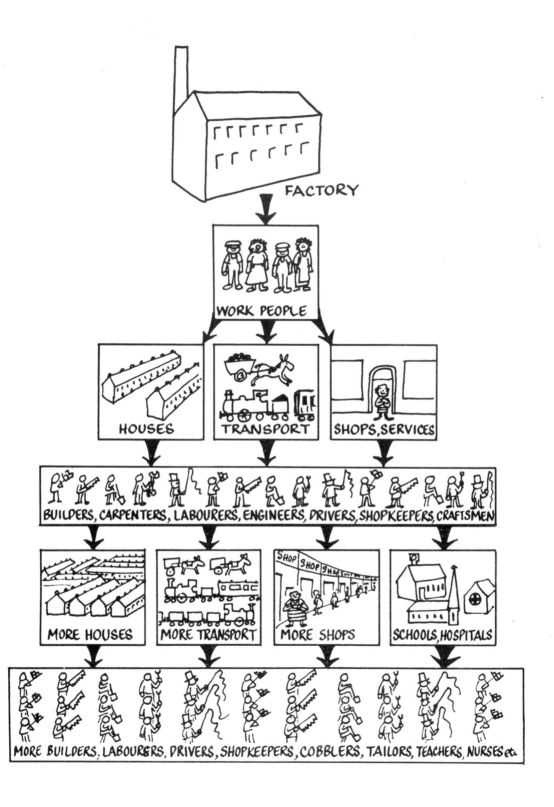

FACTORY

WORK PEOPLE

HOUSES   TRANSPORT   SHOPS, SERVICES

BUILDERS, CARPENTERS, LABOURERS, ENGINEERS, DRIVERS, SHOPKEEPERS, CRAFTSMEN

MORE HOUSES   MORE TRANSPORT   MORE SHOPS   SCHOOLS, HOSPITALS

MORE BUILDERS, LABOURERS, DRIVERS, SHOPKEEPERS, COBBLERS, TAILORS, TEACHERS, NURSES etc.

View of typical industrial slum showing courts.

Plan of a court and two rows of houses.

Cross section of one court house.

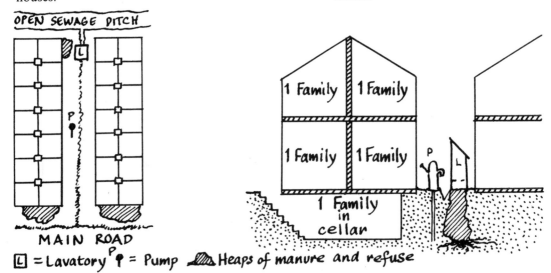

neighbourhood pour their contents into the centre of the main street. . . . Families live in the cellars and kitchens of these undrained houses, dark and extremely damp. . . . "

Here is part of another government report (1842) dealing with poorer houses in Leeds.

" . . . broken panes in every window frame, and filth and vermin in every nook. With the walls unwhitewashed for years, black with the smoke of foul chimneys, without water . . . and sacking for bed-

74

clothing, with floors unwashed from year to year, without out-offices [lavatories—the refuse would be thrown in the street]. Outside there are streets, raised a foot, sometimes two above the level of the causeway, by the accumulation of years . . . stagnant puddles here and there . . . ash-places choked up with filth, and excrementitious deposits on all sides as a consequence, undrained, unpaved, unventilated, uncared-for by any authority but the landlord, who weekly collects his miserable rents from his miserable tenants."

Most of these slums had no water supply at all except wells, pumps or, more often, the ponds and ditches into which the waste and sewage flowed. Disease spread like wildfire through the crowded hovels, and the workers, already weakened by long hours of toil in unhealthy factories and by lack of decent food, frequently died at a very early age. Compare these figures showing the average age of death in Manchester and in Rutland (a farming district) in 1842. Note carefully not only the difference between the average age of death in town and country, but also between the wealthy class and working class. A rich man in Manchester lived, on average, more than twice as long as a working man.

WEALTHY CLASS   MIDDLE CLASS   WORKING CLASS

Life for the poor was not only shorter, but it was very much harder. Often one family of six or more people lived in each room of the slum houses. The only heating would be a crude open fireplace on which any cooking had to be done. Water was stored in a bucket or an old barrel in one corner of the room to allow some of the filth to settle before it was used. Often in the opposite corner was another bucket which served as the family lavatory. The waste from this, and other household rubbish was either thrown into the street or else stored in a heap outside the door until there was enough to sell to a farmer as manure.

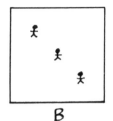

A

B

These two squares each represent one tenth of an acre—that is, a piece of land 22 yards by 22 yards. Each figure represents one person living in that area. Square **A** shows the population density in a typical industrial slum (500 or more people to the acre) and square **B** a typical modern 'new' town such as Harlow, Crawley or Peterlee (20/30 people per acre).

Furniture was often limited to a rough table, a bed in one corner, perhaps a few hard chairs or stools and boxes serving as food stores and wardrobe. A straw mattress under the table and perhaps another along one of the walls provided sleeping room for those who could not squeeze into the main bed. In 1842 an investigation into working class homes in Bury, Lancashire, found the following figures about sleeping arrangements.

> 400 families slept 1 in a bed
> 1500 families slept 2 in a bed
> 770 families slept 3 in a bed
> 210 families slept 4 in a bed
> 63 families slept 5 or more in a bed.

If you add to these discomforts the rats, the lice, the fleas and other vermin that swarmed everywhere; the damp that soaked through every wall; the overcrowding and the disease and noise, it is little wonder that these slum dwellers, when they did have a few hours free from work, hurried straight to the nearest public house (which opened as early as 5 a.m. and stayed open all day until after midnight) where for a few pence they could forget their miseries. In 1833 Manchester, with a population of 240,000, had about 1,500 inns and beerhouses. Today a town of this size (Brighton and Hove) has fewer than 200.

In the smaller and older towns things were better, though even then there was rarely any water, sanitation or paving. The very worst conditions existed in London and in the industrial towns of the midlands and the north, though some better streets and houses were built for artisans and the middle classes.

An industrial city was often divided into definite zones. In the centre was the mass of factories and slums, and beyond this there was usually a ring of better, terraced houses where the more highly paid workmen such as engineers, skilled craftsmen and clerical workers lived. These homes varied considerably. The poorer ones were not a great deal better than the slums while the best ones were very comfortable indeed. A

How the population of an industrial town might be divided.

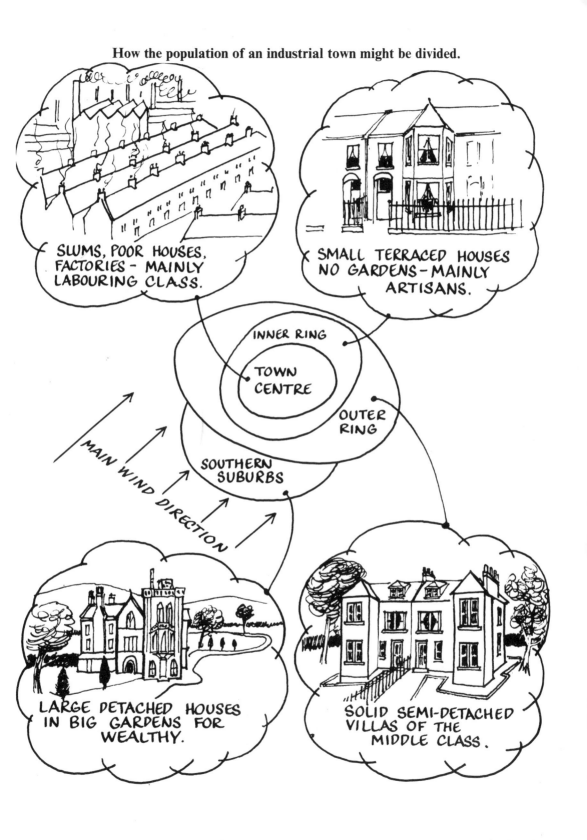

SLUMS, POOR HOUSES, FACTORIES – MAINLY LABOURING CLASS.

SMALL TERRACED HOUSES NO GARDENS – MAINLY ARTISANS.

INNER RING

TOWN CENTRE

OUTER RING

MAIN WIND DIRECTION

SOUTHERN SUBURBS

LARGE DETACHED HOUSES IN BIG GARDENS FOR WEALTHY.

SOLID SEMI-DETACHED VILLAS OF THE MIDDLE CLASS.

typical house would probably have a living room, a kitchen, two bed-rooms and an extension at the rear containing the wash-house and the lavatory and coal-house, all of which were reached from the outside. There was often a small walled yard at the back where washing was dried and the tin bath and other oddments were kept.

In the better areas cold water might be laid on to the kitchen but in the majority of houses there was either a hand pump, or else a standpipe in the street outside. A few of the more prosperous dwellings might even have water closets, but it was more usual to use cesspits, or bucket lavatories which were emptied by men who came round the streets at night with special carts.

The streets of artisans' houses improved steadily as they stretched away from the centre of the city until they merged into the outer ring where middle classes lived. Here too the buildings varied, ranging from the three-bedroom terraced homes of the lower middle class, through the semi-detached villas in their small gardens, to the large, detached houses of the prosperous shopkeepers, doctors and lawyers. Nearly all of these had mains water and, at least towards the end of the century, indoor sanitation. It was only the largest, however, which had bathrooms.

Finally, on the very outskirts of the town in what was then almost the countryside, were the sprawling, elaborate mansions of the wealthy factory owners and business men. These were usually on the southern side to escape the worst of the smoke and dust from the city. Each house stood in its own grounds set with trees, lawns and a semi-circular gravel drive leading to the front door. Every luxury that money would obtain in decoration and for convenience was lavished on them. Behind the turretted, battlemented, carved and stained-glass frontage there was running water, flush lavatories, bathrooms, gas lighting and, when it became available, electricity and the telephone.

If you live in one of the older cities, see if your town was planned on these lines. You may find it difficult to trace as many of the slums have gone, many of the upper class mansions have been pulled down to make way for blocks of flats, and huge housing estates have been built on the outskirts.

Changes in towns in the nineteenth century (see page 70)
The towns were really the creation of the nineteenth century. In 1801 only eight towns in England, Wales and Scotland had more than 50,000 inhabitants (Birmingham, Bristol, Edinburgh, Glasgow, Leeds, Liverpool, London, Manchester). In 1899 there were over 60. But quite apart from the size there were many other differences between towns, even small ones, at the beginning and end of the century.

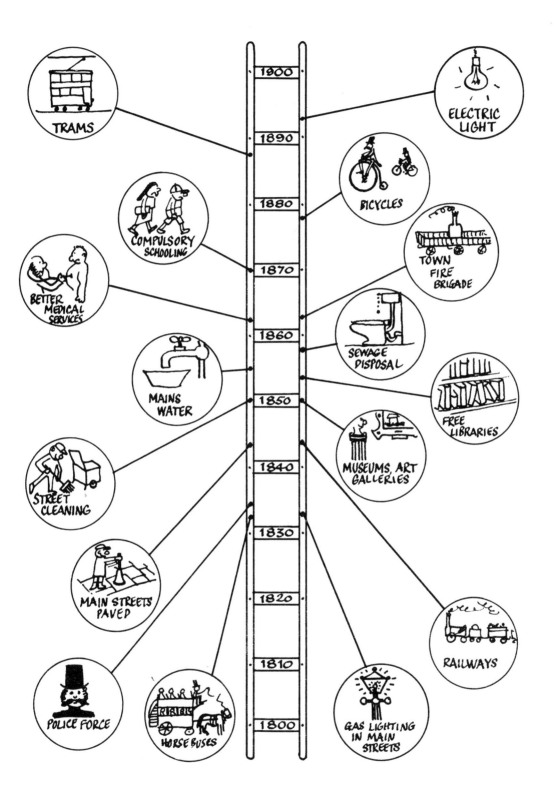

In 1800 only a few streets in London and one or two other cities had hard surfaces: the rest were of hard-packed mud with stones and gravel. Still fewer streets had any form of street lighting, and those that did, had only oil lamps which gave a faint glow for a few feet round each post. In the rest, except where the candles in a shop window threw a little light, there was complete darkness. In this gloom criminals of all types could roam freely, for not only were they protected by the night, but also they had little fear of arrest because no regular police force existed.

At the beginning of the century only the most fashionable streets in large cities were ever cleaned: 99 out of every 100 had to wait until a downpour of rain swept the rubbish into the gutter which ran along the centre. Wealthy people, for fear of robbers or filth, crossed the towns in their carriages or, until about 1810, in sedan chairs. Ordinary people walked, carrying a stout stick and a flaming torch at night to protect themselves from thieves, and wearing wooden blocks on their feet to keep themselves out of the mud and water.

In London and the smart towns like Bath, Harrogate and Tunbridge Wells there were libraries and perhaps art galleries, but the cost of admission made sure that only the 'upper' class patronised them. London and a few other towns had pleasure gardens, but again the entrance fee kept the poorer people out. For them there were few amusements except the inn, a public execution and street entertainers.

Larger houses may have had a piped water supply, and lavatories that emptied into great pits underneath the building, but the humbler people had to carry their water from the nearest well, river, ditch or pond, or if they were lucky, from the conduit, which was a kind of public fountain. Sewage and rubbish would be stacked outside the door in the street or on the nearest piece of waste ground, where it bred disease and encouraged rats.

Most large towns had doctors and a hospital of sorts, but their standards were often so low that it was only as a last resort that people asked for medical treatment. There were schools, too, but no-one was compelled to attend, and in any case, the buildings would have taken only a small fraction of the children. Schooling was expensive, or if it was cheap enough for the children of ordinary working people, it was often so bad that it was not worth having.

The towns ran few services, and left even such an important one as firefighting in the hands of the insurance companies. Each firm had its own engine, and householders were given the badge of the company with which they were insured to nail on the outside wall so that the correct engine could be called in case of a blaze. One company would fight another's fire if necessary, but they were not very willing to do so and charged heavily for their very feeble service.

During the nineteenth century most of these evils were remedied at

80

least in the larger towns. The chart on page 79 shows when these improvements began to appear in the biggest and more progressive places: smaller towns and the poorer streets of the bigger ones often had to wait 20, 30 or even 40 years for the new amenities to reach them. Even today, there are still areas without electricity and tens of thousands of homes without a proper supply of water and decent sanitation.

---

1. Explain why the richer people lived as far from the centre of Town as possible.
2. Write an account in your own words of Town Life as it is described in this chapter.
3. Describe a slum clearance project at present taking place in your city (there is bound to be one!). Find out what you can about the houses that are being demolished. How far do they fall short of modern standards of accommodation?

5

NINETEENTH CENTURY SOCIETY

The famous Victorian prime minister Benjamin Disraeli shocked the country around the middle of the century by telling the world that Britain was made up of two nations, the rich and the poor. He was, of course, exaggerating, but there was some truth in what he said. There were a few rich who were far too rich, and very many poor who were far too poor. A wealthy nobleman might have an income of £100,000 a year while a labourer often earned less than £50. Instead of Disraeli's two nations, however, society was more like a pyramid with the labouring class, who formed perhaps one third of the population, at the bottom and the aristocracy at the top. In between came the artisans, who earned between £75 and £150 a year, and then the middle classes whose income ranged from £150 to £500 or more.

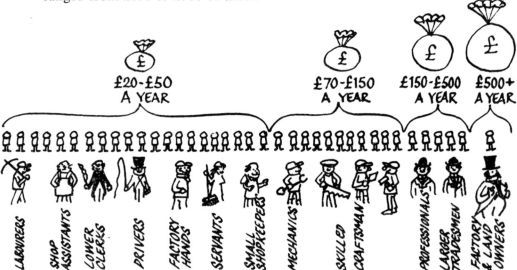

Today most of us make friends with other people who have similar interests to our own, whatever their position or job. We may well invite to a party an architect, a bank clerk, a carpenter, a doctor, an engineer and a factory worker, and no one would consider it at all unusual. Yet in Victorian times such a gathering would have been most unusual

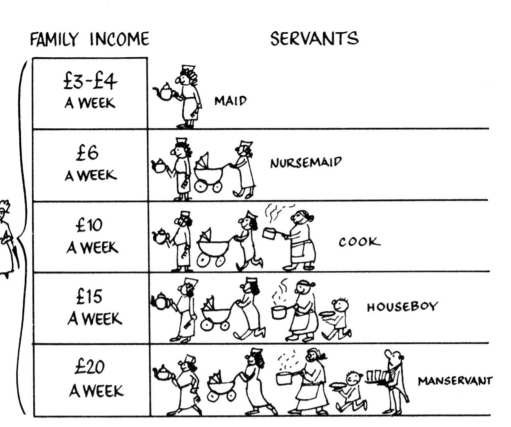

FAMILY INCOME	SERVANTS
£3-£4 A WEEK	MAID
£6 A WEEK	NURSEMAID
£10 A WEEK	COOK
£15 A WEEK	HOUSEBOY
£20 A WEEK	MANSERVANT

These figures, taken from a book published in 1861, show how much wages and values have changed. In 1967 the average wage for the working man's family was about £16. A hundred years ago a person earning this amount could have employed four servants. You might ask your parents how they would manage with a general maid, a nurse maid, a cook and a house boy.

because the classes kept very much to themselves. The artisans thought themselves to be 'above' the labouring class; the middle class considered themselves superior to the artisans, while the 'upper' class generally looked down on everyone. Even inside each class, especially the middle and upper, there were strict divisions: a prosperous shopkeeper or a senior clerk would be unlikely to be invited to a doctor's house, and the doctor himself might not be considered quite 'right' at a barrister's dinner party. In the upper class distinctions were even finer: if a person happened to live on the unfashionable side of a street, or did not have the number of servants that it was considered he should have or had a daughter who had disgraced the family by becoming an actress, he could well be shut out of the 'best' houses.

The whole situation was complicated even further by the Victorian distinction between 'wealth' and 'breeding'. A lazy, stupid, penniless scrounger who happened to be the second cousin of a duke could move

THE RICH		a. THE ARISTOCRACY b. THE NEWLY-RICH FACTORY OWNERS & BUSINESSMEN.
UPPER MIDDLE CLASS		SENIOR PROFESSIONALS — JUDGES, BANKERS, VERY RICH TRADESMEN, FASHION-ABLE DOCTORS etc.

LOWER MIDDLE CLASS — LOWER PROFESSIONAL PEOPLE, RICHER TRADESMEN.

THE ARTISAN CLASS — MECHANICS, ENGINEERS SKILLED CRAFTSMEN SENIOR CLERKS.

THE LABOURING CLASS — LABOURERS, FACTORY WORKERS, SHOP ASSISTANTS, FARMWORKERS, LOWER CLERKS etc.

THE SOCIAL PYRAMID

in the very highest levels of society while a hard-working, benevolent millionaire who had made a fortune in industry and had risen from a humble family might well be kept out. To get one's money through owning large areas of land, even if squalid slums, was considered quite respectable: to earn it in commerce as a banker or merchant was thought to be much inferior, while to have made a fortune by owning a factory or through trade was quite impossible for a 'gentleman'.

As the century progressed this rigid class system began to break down a little, though not very much. Many 'noble' families had become relatively poor and were glad to marry their sons and daughters to the children of the wealthy manufacturers and industrialists whom they had considered so much below them socially. Men who had worked their way up from poor homes to own factories and fortunes often sent their sons to the expensive public schools to mix with the sons of the 'gentry'. Here they learned the manners which, together with their fathers' wealth, enabled them to step in one generation from the bottom of the pyramid to the top.

Shops, business, industry, trade, engineering and science all offered to men who were prepared to work hard a chance of rising in the world. Better education, too, opened the door to a few children of the working

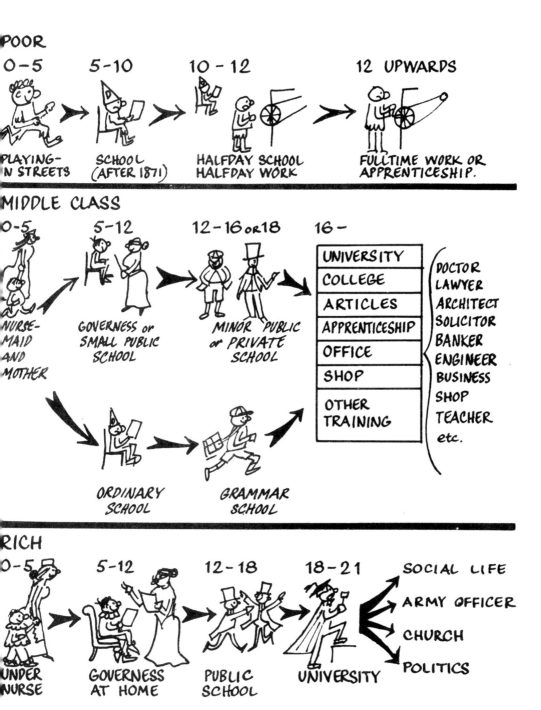

POOR

0-5	5-10	10-12	12 UPWARDS
PLAYING-IN STREETS	SCHOOL (AFTER 1871)	HALFDAY SCHOOL HALFDAY WORK	FULLTIME WORK OR APPRENTICESHIP.

MIDDLE CLASS

0-5 | 5-12 | 12-16 or 18 | 16-

NURSE-MAID AND MOTHER

GOVERNESS or SMALL PUBLIC SCHOOL

MINOR PUBLIC or PRIVATE SCHOOL

| UNIVERSITY |
| COLLEGE |
| ARTICLES |
| APPRENTICESHIP |
| OFFICE |
| SHOP |
| OTHER TRAINING |

DOCTOR
LAWYER
ARCHITECT
SOLICITOR
BANKER
ENGINEER
BUSINESS
SHOP
TEACHER
etc.

ORDINARY SCHOOL

GRAMMAR SCHOOL

RICH

0-5	5-12	12-18	18-21	
UNDER NURSE	GOVERNESS AT HOME	PUBLIC SCHOOL	UNIVERSITY	SOCIAL LIFE / ARMY OFFICER / CHURCH / POLITICS

class to enter a professional career, but even at the end of the century there was nothing like the equal opportunities that exist today.

85

The great range of wealth and position meant there there were much greater differences in the ways in which people lived in the nineteenth century than there are today. Most of us spend our lives in a similar way, but in the nineteenth century this was not so, as these diagrams show.

The poor boy started school at the age of five or six, often in a class of sixty or eighty. When he was ten (eleven after 1891) he was allowed to spend half the day at school and the other half at work. At twelve he usually gave up school altogether for full-time work, but at the end of the century the leaving age was raised to 13. If the boy was really anxious to get ahead he might be able to attend a night school if he was lucky enough to live in a town where these were held.

The rich baby on the other hand was pampered by a series of nurses from birth, and often saw his parents for only an hour a day, usually after tea. When he was five a governess was appointed to take charge of his education, but as the young gentleman had by this time learned that he was a master and she only a servant, this schooling was often rather sketchy.

At the age of about twelve the boy went to one of the public schools where he met several hundred others with backgrounds similar to his own. Here there were few servants to be cheeked and bullied so that the boys worked out their spite on each other.

After school came the university—Oxford or Cambridge—where the young man was not really expected to work very hard at his studies, but was expected to enjoy himself, preparing for the life that lay ahead.

When he left the university he was not compelled to work for his living, but if he felt that he must do something he would probably become an army officer, or enter the church or politics as these were the only careers considered suitable for 'gentlemen'. More than likely, however, he would settle down to the social life of the time, which was mainly concerned with finding enough pleasure to fill each day. These two charts show how a typical rich man and a typical poor man might spend one year of their lives.

The main season of the year was in May, June and July when everybody of importance moved to their London home for the season of balls, theatres, parties and dinners. The upper set moved steadily from mansion to mansion throughout the early summer months, eating, dancing, gossiping and flirting.

At the end of July some of the families went to the select seaside resorts, at first in Britain, but when the middle and later the working classes began to visit these places, on the continent. Some went to the country for a rest before the next gay social season of their year.

This was the busy shooting time in September and October, when the wealthy moved northwards to their Scottish homes or hotels to kill grouse, pheasants or stags. After a healthy day stalking the moors and

THE RICH – THE SOCIAL ROUND

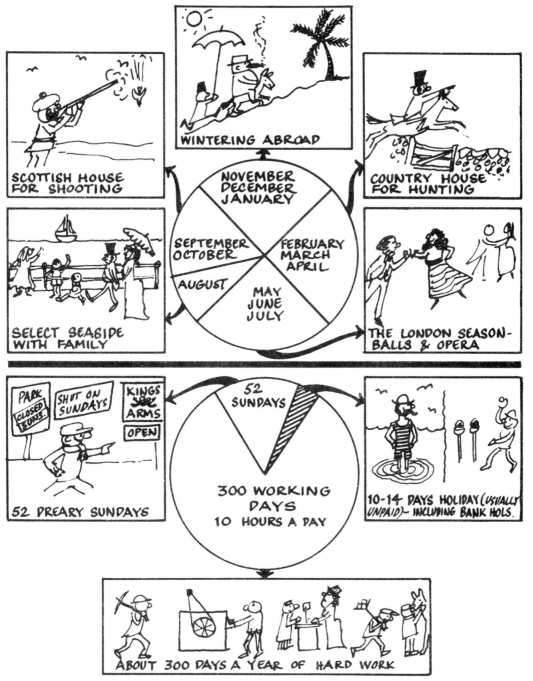

WINTERING ABROAD

SCOTTISH HOUSE FOR SHOOTING

COUNTRY HOUSE FOR HUNTING

SELECT SEASIDE WITH FAMILY

THE LONDON SEASON – BALLS & OPERA

NOVEMBER DECEMBER JANUARY

SEPTEMBER OCTOBER

FEBRUARY MARCH APRIL

AUGUST

MAY JUNE JULY

52 SUNDAYS

300 WORKING DAYS
10 HOURS A DAY

PARK CLOSED SUNS.
SHUT ON SUNDAYS
KINGS ARMS OPEN

52 DREARY SUNDAYS

10-14 DAYS HOLIDAY (USUALLY UNPAID) – INCLUDING BANK HOLS.

ABOUT 300 DAYS A YEAR OF HARD WORK

THE POOR – THE DREARY CIRCLE

hills they enjoyed another round of dinners and dances in the evenings. This continued until November when the Scottish homes, like the London houses, were shut up and left in the care of a couple of servants while the family moved abroad to a warmer climate for the coldest months of the year.

Some, however, went straight from Scotland to their country estates in the midlands and south of England for the fox hunting season which began in November. After long days in the saddle there was another round of dinners, dances and parties in the evening. Then, when the hunting ended in the spring, another London season was upon them with a round of even bigger balls, more expensive dinners and more extravagant parties.

There were, of course, many wealthy people who were very different and who genuinely devoted themselves to real work as soldiers, politicians, churchmen, lawyers, doctors and lecturers in universities. Others became famous as the heads of great businesses and commercial and banking concerns. Some spent their lives almost entirely on their country estates running the farms and improving all aspects of agriculture. A larger group still gave their lives and often a great deal of their money to one special personal interest such as social work, science, art, archaeology, engineering or exploring, and the time and energy these men spent on their chosen activity would frequently have made the hardest-worked labourer shudder.

The working class also followed a circle, but theirs was a dreary one. Of the 365 days in the year, the working man spent about 300 in his factory or other job. There would be 52 Sundays on which, of course, all places of amusement were closed. For much of the century parks, museums, art galleries and gardens were locked on the only day the poorer people were free to go to them as the upper classes did not wish to have their pleasures contaminated by the lower orders. Towards the end of the century this attitude relaxed but in the winter, especially when the weather made walks in the park or countryside impossible, the choice on Sunday lay in the public house, the church or staying at home reading.

The middle class, as always, filled the wide gap between the richest and poorest levels of society. At the upper end, a middle class boy's life would be little different from that of an aristocrat except that perhaps he would go to one of the newer and less famous schools. After school, instead of attending university, he might train at a hospital or one of the other professional schools, enter the family business or be articled to a solicitor. At the lower end a boy would probably spend five years at a grammar school which, for most of the nineteenth century, would take anyone who could pay the fees. At sixteen he would be apprenticed, go into his father's shop or settle himself in a professional man's office.

88

The wealthier middle-class man had a large house in the suburbs with a staff of several servants, and perhaps a cottage in the country where he could spend weekends and ride occasionally with the hounds. He would own several horses and a carriage and if he was not invited to have dinner at the best houses he might from time to time, if he was important enough, be asked to come later in the evening for the music or dancing. He would spend many hours at the office or consulting room but his work, though hard and exhausting, would be reasonably pleasant. Each summer he would spend a month at a rented seaside house with his family, or perhaps a few weeks at one of the nearer continental resorts. Altogether his life was probably the happiest of all: he had many of the comforts of the upper classes, but unlike them, his busy working life made sure that he did not suffer from the boredom that so often made the richest people's lives a misery.

The lower end of the middle class still enjoyed a reasonably comfortable life. Their hours were long and sometimes dreary but their home would be a pleasant villa where the mistress had the help of at least a housemaid. There would be few dinners or parties, but instead friends met at church and chapel gatherings, at public lectures and occasionally at the theatre. Usually there was a fortnight's holiday a year, which was often spent at a boarding house at the seaside.

But life for almost everyone improved in the last twenty years of the century. Every working man had at least the four bank holidays and many more were being given a week's or a fortnight's holiday a year, though rarely with pay. Shop assistants were compelled by law to have one half day free each week. A thrifty family might save for a week at the seaside in the summer or at least a trip by train to stay with relatives. There were more goods in the shops; food was better; travel was easier: Disraeli's 'two nations' were beginning to merge slightly in the centre, but even he, in his wildest dreams, would not have imagined how little difference there was to be between the factory hand and the earl in less than a hundred years.

Fashions in the nineteenth century

When we think about clothing in the nineteenth century we must not imagine rows of shops filled with a wide range of ready-made garments and shoes at reasonable prices as there are today. Nor must we think of fashions changing every year, for until the sewing machine really became efficient in the 1860s everything had to be made by hand. This meant that clothing was expensive and styles usually lasted for a number of years with only small changes.

Wealthy people chose their materials at the cloth merchant's and

1880 - 90

1860's

1800 - 15

then had them made up by dressmakers or tailors. Poorer people bought cheaper, hard-wearing plain material and usually made their own everyday garments. For 'best', if they were lucky enough to have more than one outfit, they often bought secondhand clothing which had been cast off by the upper classes and found its way to one of the scores of tiny back street stalls or shops specialising in old clothes.

In the last quarter of the century, when machinery began to be used

90

in the clothing industry, ready-made garments began to appear so that the less well-off could dress in simple, cheaper imitations of the most recent fashions. Many wealthy ladies, however, employed dressmakers until well into the twentieth century, and it was not until well into the century—the age of Burton's, Marks and Spencer and the great chain stores—that any real social levelling in people's wear began to be seen.

The style of everyday clothes for ordinary people did not change much for the whole period. Normally the men wore some form of trousers, waistcoat, shirt and jacket, and the women long, rather shapeless dresses in coarse, dark material, often with a shawl round their shoulders. If we want to see how fashions developed we must look to the wealthy class and here there was a surprising change. For the first fifteen years of the century men wore gay, brightly-coloured, rather fancy clothing, while the women wore extremely simple styles, usually in pale colours. For the rest of the century men's clothing became plainer and plainer in style, and duller and duller in colour, while the women's became more elaborate and more fussy. In the end their dresses, coats and hats were crawling with buttons, ribbons, tucks, laces, fur, feathers and ornaments of all kinds.

Until about 1815 the fashionable man dressed as you see in the illustration, perhaps with a bright blue coat, a canary-yellow waistcoat, white breeches and black boots. Beards were not popular, but the smart young man had thick, bushy sideboards. Women dressed in what they thought was an imitation of the dress of Roman and Greek women. Their dresses were usually made of a very thin material such as muslin gathered in to a 'waist' just below the armpits. From here the skirt fell straight to the ground, rather like a modern long nightdress—in fact the 'Empire' line, as it was called, did look very much like a nightdress with sleeves. Underneath they sometimes wore a kind of petticoat called a shift, but the really fashionable lady had nothing—underwear at the time was considered rather indecent.

After 1815 dresses became thicker, fuller and lower in the waist with underwear in the shape of long pantaloons. Ladies struggled to outdo each other in the fullness of their skirts, padding them out first with underskirts and later with cushions until, about the middle of the century, the crinoline arrived. This was a wire or wooden framework something like an umbrella frame which fastened round the waist. The skirts were spread over this until sometimes the dresses were five or six feet in diameter. Three or four women completely filled a large room, and trying to pass along a busy shopping street was a serious problem for a man. As the crinolines swayed from side to side in the wind or when the wearer moved, the ladies wore high, laced-up boots to prevent anyone catching a glimpse of their ankles—a sight which the Victorians thought rather indecent.

91

A lady dresses—about 1860.

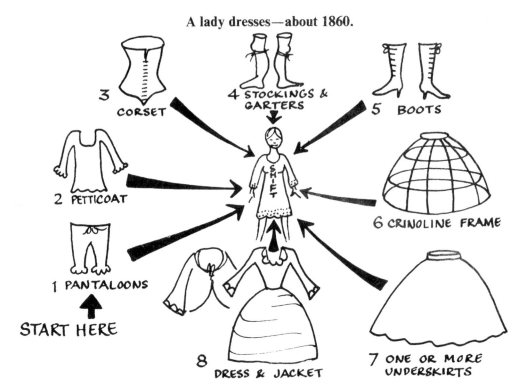

3 CORSET

4 STOCKINGS & GARTERS

5 BOOTS

2 PETTICOAT

6 CRINOLINE FRAME

1 PANTALOONS

START HERE

8 DRESS & JACKET

7 ONE OR MORE UNDERSKIRTS

By this time men had developed a dress not very different from that of our own except that the jackets were longer and buttoned nearly from top to bottom. The collars were very high and a cravat was worn instead of a tie. Beards and moustaches, the bigger and curlier the better, were very popular. Suits were usually in dark, plain colours, but on informal occasions a quiet stripe in the trousers might be allowed.

It was at this time too that tiny waists became the height of fashion with ladies. A very smart woman would aim at sixteen inches, though a few managed to squeeze down to fourteen or even twelve inches. If you want to see just how small this is, take a strip of paper sixteen inches long and form it into a loop.

As nature had not provided ladies with measurements like these, they had to use strong corsets which laced up at the back. The maid would pull the cords, gradually squashing in her mistress's stomach half-inch by half-inch until it would go no further. Not only was this very uncomfortable, but also it was very dangerous to health, for the wearer could not breathe properly and her intestines were pushed into unnatural positions. The Victorian lady's habit of fainting so frequently may well have been due to the tight lacing of corsets which did not allow her enough air.

After about 1870 the crinoline went out of fashion and the hump

92

Main hairstyles of the nineteenth century.

1820's   **1850's**   **1880's**

1820   **1850**   **1890**

moved to the back to form the bustle. Women were now 'S' shaped if viewed from the side, and although this had to be formed by strong corsets again, fortunately the very small waists dropped out of fashion. To crown this odd figure was an immense hat, sometimes three feet across, decorated with anything from stuffed birds to baskets of fruit.

Men's clothing had almost reached modern styles except that they were much duller in colour and the jackets still buttoned up very high. Collars were very stiff and tall, and the top hat or bowler was worn by most older men in town. In the country or for cycling, however, the Norfolk jacket and breeches were popular, especially with younger men. Here a few prices of clothing and material taken from a weekly magazine for the middle and upper classes in 1879.

> **Cotton dress material** . . . from 4¾d a yard.
> **Sound wool serge material** . . . from 6¾d a yard.
> **Flannel** . . . 8¾d a yard.
> **Silk velvet** . . . 2/11½d a yard.
> **Large towels** . . . 6/9d a dozen.
> **Men's shirts** . . . from 30/– for 6.
> **Gloves** . . . 1/2½d a pair.
> **Chemises** (petticoats) . . . 4/6d for 3.
> **Long nightdresses** . . . 8/6d for 3.
> **Tucked and trimmed ladies drawers** (long) . . . 4/6d for 3.
> **Evening dresses** . . . from £1 1s 0d.
> **Corsets, fashionable shape** . . . 2/11½d to 4/11d.

In the same magazine the famous London furniture firm of Maples and Company were advertising bedroom suites from £6·83 and bedsteads from 43p.

All of these show just how much machinery had brought down the cost of everyday articles. Many toilet items and medicines were, however, still made at home. Here are a few recipes taken from Mrs Beeton's *Household Management,* first published in the 1860s. The servants were expected to make these up for the use of their mistresses or in the house.

AN EXCELLENT POMATUM [Hair oil]

$1\frac{1}{2}$ lb lard $\qquad$ $\frac{1}{2}$ pint olive oil
$\frac{1}{2}$ pint castor oil $\qquad$ 4 oz scent
elder-flower water.

All the ingredients were mixed together with a little brandy—and a revolting hair cream it must have been.

A PASTE TO RESTORE WHITENESS TO LINEN WHICH HAS BEEN SCORCHED

$\frac{1}{2}$ pint vinegar, 2 oz fuller's-earth, 1 oz dried fowls' dung,
$\frac{1}{4}$ oz soap, the juice of two large onions.

The ingredients were boiled together to form a paste and then spread on the scorch mark.

Education

At the beginning of the century perhaps not more than three children out of every ten went to school for there was no law saying that they must do so. More and more of them were going into the factories and mines that were developing in the midlands and north of the country.

Perhaps they did not miss much, for few of those who did attend school received anything that we would call education. Some went to the old grammar schools, most of which were now very bad indeed and taught mainly Latin and Greek; some went to the charity schools which had been set up by wealthy merchants; some went to dame schools where for a penny or two a week an old man or woman, often illiterate themselves, tried to teach them simple arithmetic and the alphabet, and some went to Sunday schools where the aim was to learn to read the Bible.

As the Industrial Revolution began to spread it was obvious that more and more educated people were needed. Engineers and scientists were needed to design and build machines, and this needed a good grasp of mathematics; mechanics were needed to repair and run the machines and this demanded at least the ability to read instructions; far more clerks were needed to deal with business letters and accounts, and even factory workers had to be able to understand notices.

The first step towards an educational system came at the beginning of the century when two church societies set up schools in many parts of the country. They had to do this as cheaply as possible and they devised a system whereby one master often had four or five hundred pupils all on his own. The master taught the older boys, or *monitors* as they were called, and these taught the younger ones. It was a poor system, but at least it was a step in the right direction and one could not expect much for a few pence a week.

94

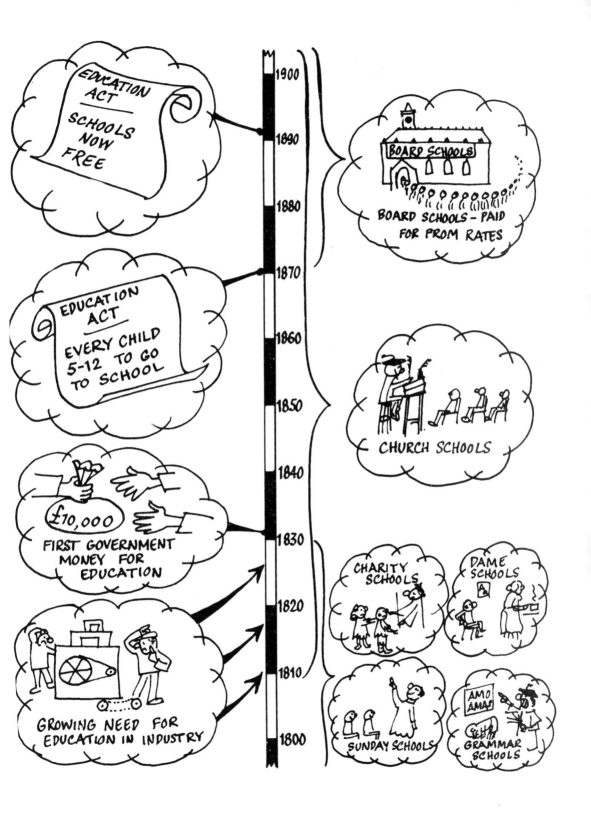

In the 1830s the government realised that it must do something about education as England was slipping far behind Scotland and other countries in Europe. It gave £10,000 to each of the church societies, and though this grant was increased in the 1840s to £100,000 a year, it was a trifling amount when you consider that well over one thousand million pounds a year is spent today on education.

By the middle of the century perhaps six or seven children out of every ten were getting some teaching, though they could start when they liked, stay as long as they liked and leave when they liked. The government saw that this was not good enough and in 1870 passed an Education Act which in effect made it compulsory for all boys and girls to attend school from the ages of 5 to 12, though they still had to pay. Where no church or charity school existed each town had to appoint a committee, or school board, which took money from local rates to build and run a school.

Although classes were large—70 pupils was a usual number—education slowly improved, and in the last ten years of the century schools were made free and the leaving age was raised to 13. You might like to make a list of the schools in your area and see which of them are still controlled, either completely or partly, by the church.

---

1. Can you account for the class divisions that existed so strictly in the early part of the nineteenth century? Why did people grade themselves into classes in the way described in this chapter?
2. What reasons can you give for the gradual merging of Disraeli's 'two nations' in the latter half of the nineteenth century?
3. What was (a) the 'Empire Line', (b) a crinoline, (c) a bustle?
4. Why was education so urgently needed in the nineteenth century? Why, today, is there an even more urgent need for it?

6

REFORM!

Changes in Parliament and in voting

Britain is one of the very few countries which have had a properly elected parliament ever since the middle ages. Although this parliament sat in London and made laws, the local nobleman or the nearest town council usually had more direct effect on the lives of the people than the government because communications between the capital and the rest of the country were so bad.

While this situation was quite satisfactory when Britain was a land of tiny villages and small towns which had little to do with one another, the different districts could no longer be allowed to go their own ways when the country became industrialised and the huge cities began to develop.

Trying to run this new, bustling industrial country put a great strain on parliament, and parliament as it was at the beginning of the nineteenth century was not fit to cope with many of the problems it had to face. One of its main weaknesses was that it no longer represented the people it was intended to represent because the method of electing M.P.s had changed little in 500 years whereas the country itself had changed enormously.

First of all, when parliament began to take shape in the thirteenth century, all of the important towns had been allowed to send two members. By the nineteenth century many places which had been important in 1265, when the first proper parliament had been called, had decayed into tiny villages or had vanished altogether. Yet these still sent two M.P.s to Westminster. The worst of these 'rotten boroughs' as they were called, were Dunwich, on the Suffolk coast, which had long since vanished beneath the waves, and Old Sarum, in Wiltshire, which was nothing more than a large mound of earth in a field.

At the opposite extreme to the tiny places with only a few dozen inhabitants which still returned members to parliament were the great new industrial cities like Manchester, Birmingham and Leeds. These had not existed, or else had been tiny, unimportant hamlets in the middle ages when parliament began and so had not been allowed any M.P.s. Although they now had populations of 100,000 or more, they were still not allowed any representatives.

Another disadvantage of the old system was that a wealthy nobleman could control a number of small villages which still sent M.P.s to London. As the villagers normally worked for the nobleman and lived in his houses, he could force them to vote for whoever he wished—often a member of his own family. In 1816, for example, the Duke of Norfolk could control 11 M.P.s, Lord Lonsdale 9 and the Duke of Newcastle 7. It was estimated that 87 dukes, earls and lords between them could return 218 members.

Even in those towns and villages that did send members to parliament by no means every man could vote. In some places only those men who lived in certain streets or even certain houses were eligible: in other places a man had to have lived for a certain number of years in the village. Some towns allowed only the town council to elect the M.P.s, while in others any man who owned a fireplace large enough to boil a pot could vote.

Finally, when it had been decided who could vote and who could not, the actual method of choosing the candidate was unfair and out-of-date. The election might last for three or four weeks and during this time a large, open-sided shed on stilts, called the hustings, was built in the centre of the town. From here the Tory or Whig candidates made their speeches, though few people heard them because the opposing side usually drowned their talk with shouting and horn blowing. Those men who did have the right to vote then had to mount the steps of the hustings and in full view of the crowd tell the official in charge which of the candidates they supported.

This open voting naturally led to much corruption. A candidate anxious to gain a seat in parliament would pay a man up to five pounds for a vote if the contest looked like being a close one. If this failed, the voter could be made drunk and then persuaded to change his mind. As a last resort, each candidate had a gang of burly hooligans to threaten the voter with a beating if he did not cast his vote as they wished.

Before the industrial revolution most people had been living in small, widely-separated villages and rarely met anyone from outside. Now, in the factories, men from all over Britain worked side by side and discussed such things as politics. They no longer had the lord of the manor watching over them and threatening them so that they felt much freer to complain. They saw much that was wrong and unjust in their home conditions, their working life and in the running of the country.

Feelings rapidly built up. Men felt that if only they had some say in choosing their government, all the cruelties, injustices and hardships would vanish. Meetings were called; strikes, disturbances and riots broke out, especially in the midlands and north of England where most of the industry had grown up.

At last Parliament gave way, and after a great struggle the Reform Act of 1832 was passed. This took away M.P.s from most of the rotten

The main changes in the 1832 Reform Act.

N'HUMBS
● ●

CUMBS
● ● ●

DURHAM
● ● ●
● ● ●

○
WESTMORLAND

YORKS
● ● ● ● ●

LANCS
● ● ● ● ●
● ● ● ●

CHESHIRE
● ● ● ●

DERBY
● ●

NOTTS
● ●

STAFFS
● ● ● ●
● ● ● ●

LEICS
● ●

NORFOLK

WORCS
● ●

WARWICK
● ● ● ●

SUFFOLK
○ ○ ○ ○ ○

GLOUCESTER
● ● ● ● ●

MIDDLESEX
● ● ● ● ●

ESSEX
● ● ● ●

GLAM
● ● ● ●

WILTSHIRE
○ ○ ○ ○
○ ○ ○ ○ ○
○ ○ ○ ○ ○
○ ○ ○ ○ ○
○ ○ ○ ○ ○

SOMERSET
○ ○ ○

HAMPSHIRE
○ ○ ○ ○
○ ○ ○

SUSSEX
○ ○ ○ ○ ○ ○ ○ ○ ○
○ ○

DEVON
○ ○

DORSET
○ ○ ○
○ ○ ○

CORNWALL
○ ○ ○ ○ ○ ○ ○
○ ○ ○ ○ ○ ○ ○
○ ○ ○
○ ○ ○

○ = LOST ONE M.P.
● = GAINED ONE M.P.

boroughs (Wiltshire and Cornwall together lost 50 M.P.s) and gave them to some of the big new industrial cities. The act also allowed more people of the middle class to vote, but it still did not allow the working men to do so, nor did it change the out-of-date method of elections at the hustings.

When the people were given the right to vote.

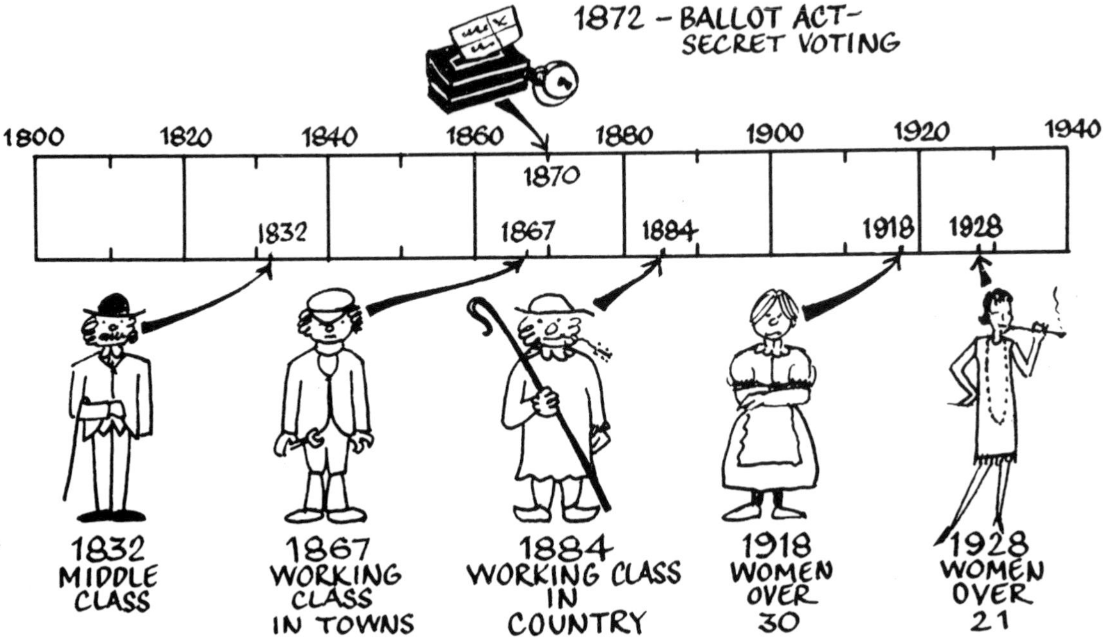

1872 – BALLOT ACT–
SECRET VOTING

1800   1820   1840   1860   1880   1900   1920   1940

1870

1832   1867   1884   1918   1928

1832
MIDDLE
CLASS

1867
WORKING
CLASS
IN TOWNS

1884
WORKING CLASS
IN
COUNTRY

1918
WOMEN
OVER
30

1928
WOMEN
OVER
21

1928 ◄— V O T E R S

1918 ◄— V O T E R S

1884 ◄ VOTERS

1867 ◄ VOTERS

1832 ◄ VOTERS

1831 ◄ VOTERS

Thirty-five years later Parliament passed a second Reform Act which gave the right to vote to working men in towns, but not in some country districts. This doubled the number of voters and it soon became obvious that the old way of choosing the M.P.s publicly was becoming quite unworkable. Secret voting on a slip of paper was introduced by the Ballot Act of 1872 so that an employer could no longer threaten his men with dismissal if they voted against his wishes.

In 1885 the vote was given to farm workers, so that by the end of the century nearly all men over the age of 21 could do so. Women still had to wait nearly thirty years before they had reached equality with men in the matter of voting, but their struggle is part of Book 4.

Crime and punishment

At the beginning of the nineteenth century a life of crime was a very easy one. If the criminal was careful there was little fear of being caught as there were no police as we know them. In London there were a few paid men, including the famous Bow Street Runners, who tried to keep law and order, but they were far too few. Many parts of the country managed with night watchmen, who were often too old and feeble to do anything else, or unpaid constables chosen from the men of the town. Every man was liable to take his turn as constable but it was such a hated job that many people paid a regular man to do their duty for them. In some places the merchants or townsfolk banded together to form a voluntary force. In others they paid watchmen out of their own pockets to guard their property.

Most of the wrong-doers unlucky enough to be arrested were caught by thief-takers, who were private citizens making a living by catching criminals for the rewards. Often these thief-takers were worse than the men they caught. They frequently planned the crime themselves and then, in the middle of the robbery arrested the men who were helping them.

When a criminal was caught, however, the law showed little mercy for people believed that if he were savagely punished it would be a warning to others. Because of this idea there were over 200 offences for which a person could be executed. These ranged from stealing a pocket handkerchief, cutting down growing trees or pretending to be a pensioner of Chelsea Hospital, to murder and treason. Men, women and children were hanged publicly and good seats on the specially-erected grandstands outside the gaol fetched high prices.

For lesser offences—say, killing a rabbit or taking turnips from a farmer's field—the prisoner could be transported for 5, 7 or 14 years. This meant a dreadful voyage in a prison cage to the new colony of

101

Australia, or later Bermuda and Gibraltar, where the convict became a slave. He worked as an unpaid servant to one of the settlers or else as a labourer in a chain gang making roads and buildings for the government. At the end of his sentence he was given a plot of land in the wilderness— 30 acres for a single man and 50 for a married one—and allowed to settle down as a farmer. Many ex-convicts, however, managed to return to England illegally, but if they were caught they were liable to be executed.

For a sentence of less than five years the prisoner was sent to one of the English gaols where conditions were extremely harsh. Convicts of all ages were packed into filthy cells without enough water, light or proper food. The gaolers were usually unpaid and made their living by hiring beds and blankets to the prisoners and by selling food, beer, tobacco and other articles. Even a man who had been found not guilty in court could be kept in prison for years by the warders because he was unable to pay them what he owed. This is part of a report on Newgate Gaol in London in 1814. The men in these cells had done no crime except being unable to pay their debts.

"No bedding is provided: the poorer description of prisoners sleep on the boards between two rugs given by the city: those who can afford it hire beds at sixpence the night. The allowance of food for debtors is 14 ounces of bread a day and eight stone of meat divided among all [this amounted to about 2 ounces a day per person]: there are no candles or coals, no mops or pails. . . . "

There were, however, cells where 'prisoners of every crime may be admitted . . . on payment of 13s 6d and 2s 6d a week for the use of a bed'.

Even better cells still were available for those who had money in what was called the 'State Side'.

'The fee for admission is two guineas, and a rent of 10s 6d for a single bed and 7s when two sleep in one bed. . . . '

The women's cells were no better, as this report shows.

"The women's yards . . . with cells . . . are calculated for seventy persons. In January last 130 were, at one time, crowded together, of all ages, all descriptions, tried and untried; and even those under sentence of death are not removed . . . amongst these are now two girls of thirteen, one of twelve and one of ten years old . . . "

Fortunately a few clear-sighted men saw that savage punishment was not the answer to crime. They realised it was much better to catch more criminals and give them light sentences than to let 99 out of every 100 escape and to punish the hundredth by execution. Some men and

102

In the 1830s, of every 8 prisoners found guilty . . .

| 1 was sentenced to death | 2 were transported | 5 were in British prisons. |

women, especially John Howard and Elizabeth Fry, realised that the terrible conditions in prisons, far from reforming the convicts, only made them worse than ever.

In 1829, Sir Robert Peel, who was then the Home Secretary, organised the first real police for London. Several thousand men, mainly ex-soldiers, were enlisted into a force, given a uniform and were paid wages instead of living on rewards. These men soon became known as 'Peelers' or 'Bobbies' after the surname or Christian name of their founder.

Crime in London fell sharply as more and more men were arrested, and soon the new force was being copied all over England. In some places the police were set up because the authorities thought they were a good idea: in others, because the criminals, finding London too dangerous, fled to parts of the country where they thought life would be easier. By the middle of the century 22 counties of England had regular police forces, and long before the end every square inch of the country was under the supervision of one policeman or another.

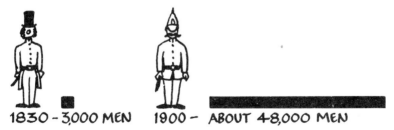

1830 – 3,000 MEN   1900 – ABOUT 48,000 MEN

During the 1820s and 1830s Robert Peel and other men who believed in his ideas began to reform the prisons. They ordered prisons to be run on a plan drawn up by the government and appointed inspectors to see that this was being carried out. Gaolers were paid wages to prevent them taking advantage of the prisoners, and the convicts were to be taught to read and write while serving their sentences. To the amazement of many

 1810 9,600 CONVICTIONS 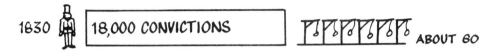 OVER 80 EXECUTIONS

1830 18,000 CONVICTIONS ABOUT 60

 1899 25,000 CONVICTIONS LESS THAN 20

who believed that the harsher the punishment the better it would be, this milder treatment led to fewer men returning to prison.

With the new police force making crime much less safe and with prisons a little less harsh than they had been, Peel and the reformers tried to persuade Parliament to make the punishments less severe. For years a bitter battle was waged over the offences for which a person could be executed, and one by one more ridiculous of these, such as damaging Westminster Bridge, were removed. After 1841 the only crimes for which hanging remained were murder and treason.

By the middle of the century only transportation remained of the old order, and as Australia began to develop, her people objected to having Britain's criminals thrown on them. The government tried other colonies, such as Bermuda, Gibraltar and Tasmania without much success, and the last of the infamous convict ships sailed in 1868. Prisoners now served their sentences in British prisons which, if still hard, uncomfortable and often cruel, were at least at home.

---

1. What was (a) a rotten borough, (b) a pocket borough?
2. Account for the fact that some of the major cities in Britain were hardly represented in Parliament while places like Dunwich and Old Sarum could return two members.
3. What events led up to the Great Reform Act of 1832? What caused ordinary men to become more politically conscious?
4. Why is a secret ballot so important in an election?
5. In history books and encyclopaedias find out what you can about the Reform Acts of the nineteenth century, and explain why people became much more concerned about the right to vote.
6. Find out what you can about (a) Bow Street runners, (b) Peelers, or the first policemen, (c) Thief Takers. Write short notes on each.
7. Find out what you can about *Transportation*.

REFORMS THAT CHANGED PEOPLE'S LIVES IN THE 19th CENTURY

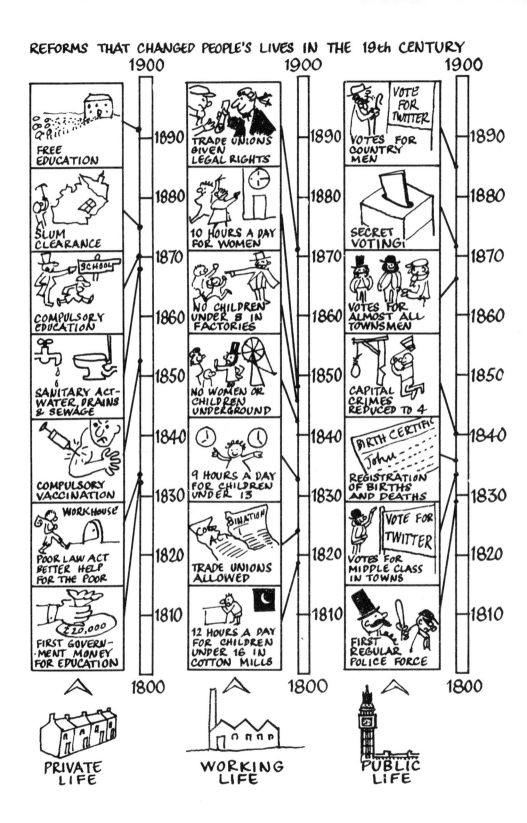

7

MEDICINE AND PUBLIC HEALTH
1800-1900

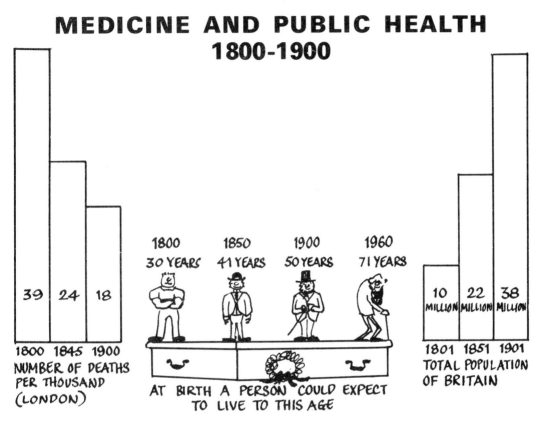

39	24	18

1800 1845 1900
NUMBER OF DEATHS
PER THOUSAND
(LONDON)

1800	1850	1900	1960
30 YEARS	41 YEARS	50 YEARS	71 YEARS

AT BIRTH A PERSON COULD EXPECT
TO LIVE TO THIS AGE

10 MILLION	22 MILLION	38 MILLION

1801 1851 1901
TOTAL POPULATION
OF BRITAIN

These charts show three remarkable changes which took place in the nineteenth century. The death rate (that is, the number of people in every thousand of the population who died each year) fell from about 39 in 1800 to 18 in 1900. The average age of dying rose from 30 to 50, and the total population of the country grew from 10 million at the first census in 1801, to 38 million in 1901. In a hundred years the population increased nearly four times, mainly because people were living longer.

There were two main causes for the steadily improving health of the people in the nineteenth century. There were great discoveries in medicine on the one hand, and a number of laws dealing with health and social conditions such as sanitation and working hours on the other.

There had been some improvement in medicine during the eighteenth century but even in 1800 it was still very primitive. Most people still made their own herbal cures and only as a very last resort sought treatment at one of the few hospitals. These were usually filthy and their attendants (one cannot really call them nurses) were normally ignorant, untrained drunkards. Patients were often herded into the same ward, whether they had a highly infectious and fatal fever or a minor broken limb. Many doctors were inefficient and operations undertaken only if it was a matter of life or death. The patient was either made blind drunk, or else strapped down on the table or held by hefty servants while the surgeon slashed him open as rapidly as possible with instruments which more than likely bore the stains of dried blood and pus from the last patient. Doctors realised that there was some connection between filth and disease, but they assumed that the unpleasant smell was the cause. It was not until the second half of the century that the existence of germs was discovered and only then did need for cleanliness become obvious.

For the first forty years of the century the health of the people, at least in the industrial towns, grew rapidly worse. The filthy drinking water, the stagnant pools of sewage and the overcrowding brought on diseases which killed the factory workers in thousands. They were already weakened so much by long hours of work in dreadful conditions and by poor food that many illnesses which today are very minor were fatal. The average age of death in one Lancashire cotton town was 17 years. Diseases such as cholera and typhoid, which are spread by sewage and drinking water becoming mixed, were present all the time, but in 1832, 1849, 1854 and 1865 the cholera plague struck Britain particularly badly, killing 53,000 people in 1832, 55,000 in 1849, 22,000 in 1854 and 18,000 in 1865. And these fevers from filth were not confined to the slums—Prince Albert, the husband of Queen Victoria, died of typhoid contracted at Windsor Castle from polluted water.

At last, however, the industrial revolution, the cause of so much poor health, began to bear useful fruits. From the mills came cheap cotton so that the working class began to wear cotton shirts, cotton trousers, cotton dresses and cotton jackets instead of the traditional woollen ones. Wool can be washed only in warm water and must never be boiled: cotton gets dirty more quickly but it can be cleaned easily by boiling. Boiling kills off any germs which collect in the fibres, whereas in woollen clothing they remained to infect the wearer and others. The new factories too began to make cheap soap so that the housewife, instead of having to make her own with fat and wood ash (which the poor rarely had time to do), could buy it from the shops. Soap is a powerful germ killer, and, although no-one at the time realised that there were such things as microbes, the wider use of soap for washing clothes and the body did help to keep down some diseases. The improvements in iron manufacture enabled towns in the second half of the century to lay water- and sewage pipes quickly and cheaply, and this, perhaps more than anything else, raised the standard of health in towns.

In the field of medicine there were three main developments, apart from Dr Jenner's discovery of vaccination in 1796. For centuries doctors had looked for a way of putting patients to sleep so that they could be spared the agony of operations. In 1846 an American, Dr Morton, used laughing gas (Nitrous oxide) to make a man unconscious while he pulled out his teeth, and the next year, Dr Simpson, a Scotsman, first used chloroform, which was a much better anaesthetic.

These two opened a completely new field in surgery, for with a patient conscious, operations had to be carried out extremely rapidly or there was a good chance of death from shock. A good surgeon, before the use of anaesthetic, could slit open a man's stomach and remove a stone from the bladder in 30–40 seconds. Now with the patient deeply asleep the doctors could take their time and probe deeper and deeper into the body.

At once the death rate rose alarmingly: the patients no longer died of shock but of blood poisoning, for the doctors operated in their ordinary clothes, on an ordinary table, with instruments they had used dozens of times without cleaning or sterilising. No antiseptic precautions were taken at all as no-one realised that there was any danger in dirt. It was not until twenty years later, in the 1860s, that the Frenchman Pasteur showed that disease was due to invisible organisms called germs which flourished in filthy conditions.

Once the enemy was known it was fairly easy to find ways of destroying it. In England, Lord Lister discovered that carbolic acid killed germs and in the late 1860s, began to use it in surgery. His apparatus consisted of a pump rather like the modern aerosol which squirted a spray of carbolic acid over the patient. At first the people undergoing the antiseptic surgery tended to die of carbolic acid poisoning instead of blood poisoning, but soon the details were perfected and the drop in the number of deaths was almost miraculous, as this chart shows.

In 1880, of every ten major amputations . . .

by the old method, 5 died, 5 lived.
By Lister's method, 1 died, 9 lived.

Once the idea of germs and antiseptics was thoroughly understood progress was rapid, and in the last years of the century disease after disease was conquered. One of the weakest links in the medical chain, however, was nursing, which, until the middle of the century was still largely regarded as a labouring job for the lowest type of woman. The great change here occurred when Florence Nightingale, who came from a very wealthy aristocratic family reorganised the nursing of wounded soldiers in the Crimean War of 1854–6. Although she was never really fit again, after her two terrible years in the military hospital in Turkey, she worked behind the scenes to make nursing a skilful and highly respected profession.

While the doctors were making their discoveries, the government was at length forced by the public into doing something. A committee was set up to find out just how the working classes lived and in 1842 it published a *Report on the Condition of the Labouring Population of Great Britain*. This report ran to almost 30 volumes and its main author, Edwin Chadwick, sums up at the end:

". . . The various forms of . . . disease are caused, or aggravated . . .

among the labouring classes by atmospheric impurities produced by decomposing animal and vegetable substances, by damp and filth, and close overcrowded dwellings. . . .

Disease . . . is always found in connection with the . . . circumstances above . . . and that where those circumstances are removed by drainage, proper cleansing, better vantilation and other means . . . the disease is abated. . . .

The annual loss of life from filth and bad ventilation is greater than the loss from death or wounds in any wars in which the country has been engaged in modern times. . . .

The greatest proportion of deaths of the heads of families occurred from the above (that is, dirt, bad sanitation, etc.) and other removable causes . . . their ages were under 45 years. . . . "

The nation was shocked by the report, but little was done as many members of Parliament were making vast fortunes from the rents of the slums. Six years later a Board of Health was set up but in the face of the powerful landowners it was able to do little. Meanwhile the plagues of cholera and typhus continued, with particularly violent epidemics of cholera in 1849 and 1854.

In 1853, however, the government did pass the first really important health measure by insisting that every baby must be vaccinated against smallpox, a disease which was responsible in 1850 for 9,900 deaths. As vaccination had been discovered nearly sixty years earlier and had been proved to be very effective, the government was certainly not hurrying itself. The epidemics of cholera at last compelled the government to

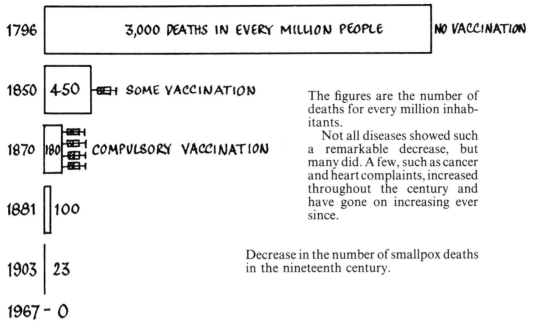

1796 — 3,000 DEATHS IN EVERY MILLION PEOPLE — NO VACCINATION

1850 — 450 — SOME VACCINATION

1870 — 180 — COMPULSORY VACCINATION

The figures are the number of deaths for every million inhabitants.

Not all diseases showed such a remarkable decrease, but many did. A few, such as cancer and heart complaints, increased throughout the century and have gone on increasing ever since.

1881 — 100

1903 — 23

Decrease in the number of smallpox deaths in the nineteenth century.

1967 - 0

take action. A Sanitary Act of 1866 forced towns which did not have a proper water supply and a sewage disposal system to instal them at once, and at the same time it made overcrowding illegal. Every town had to appoint a sanitary inspector to see that these reforms were carried out.

But no amount of piped water and sanitation would help some of the worst housing and nine years later the government passed a Housing Act. This allowed towns to pull down the worst of the slums and to build better homes for the inhabitants. Some towns, such as Birmingham, took full advantage of the Act and began clearing great areas of the city: others, unfortunately, were controlled by the owners of the slums who took good care that nothing interfered with their profits. Unfortunately even new houses can quickly become slums so that the problem of bad housing is with us still, almost a century after the Housing Act.

Gradually, however, conditions of health improved in the last thirty years of the century.

The discoveries in medicine and the government's laws concerning sanitation and housing were greatly helped by an improvement in the food of the working people. Railways could bring fresh fish and milk to the cities: fast steamboats brought fruit and vegetables from abroad: refrigeration (after the 1880s) enabled meat to be brought from Australia, Argentina, New Zealand and America at about half the cost of home-produced beef and mutton; tinned meat and fruit appeared after 1870 and packeted foods began to make life easier for the housewife. Although there was still desperate poverty and filthy housing conditions, and although in the last years of the century about 24,000 people died each

111

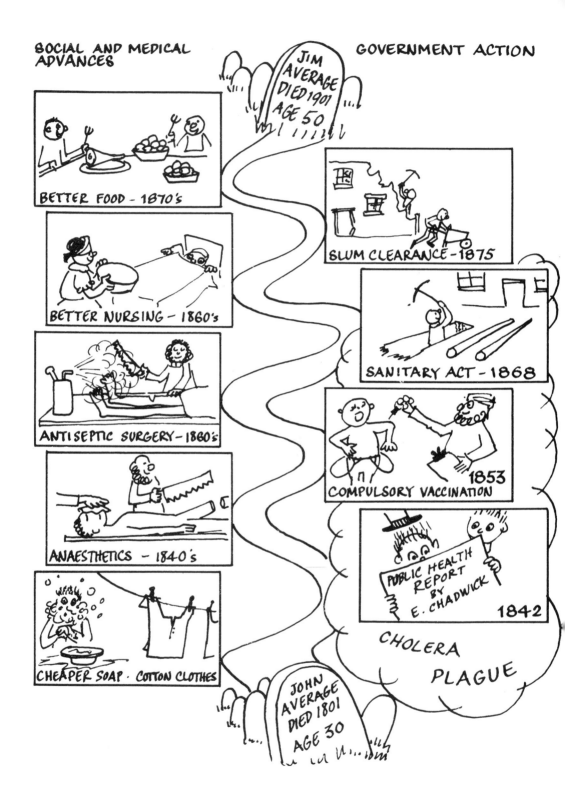

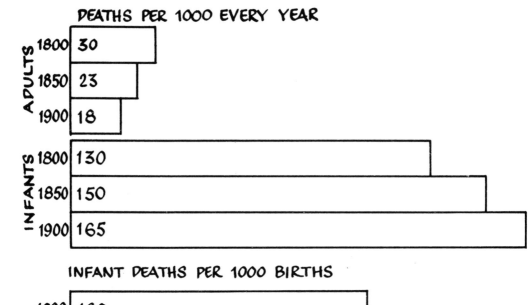

DEATHS PER 1000 EVERY YEAR

ADULTS

1800	30
1850	23
1900	18

INFANTS

1800	130
1850	150
1900	165

INFANT DEATHS PER 1000 BIRTHS

1899	160
1920	82
1940	61
1964	20

year of scarlet fever (in 1962 only two people died of this disease); 15,000 died of whooping cough (in 1962—34); 11,000 died of measles (in 1962—50); and 3,000 of diphtheria (in 1962—2), the country was a much healthier place than it had been in its history.

The health of children

These surprising charts show that while the death rates for adults dropped sharply in the nineteenth century, the rate for children actually increased to the appalling figure of 165 per 1,000 in 1900, in spite of all the medical advances. And this figure was an average for the country as a whole: in the industrial slums it was much worse. In York, for example, it was 250 per 1,000 in 1900—that is, *one quarter* of the children born died. A typical Victorian family had twelve children, so that in the bad areas one could expect at least two or three of these to die as babies.

Much of this dreadful loss of life was due to ignorance and bad conditions in the homes. The houses were often filthy—in the 1880s over 12,000 babies a year died of diarrhoea caused mainly by dirt.

113

5

Overcrowding in the poorer homes, with families of ten or more in three or four rooms, made sure that any infectious disease spread rapidly. There was generally no free medical treatment so that parents tried their own remedies and because of the expense often put off calling in a doctor until it was too late.

Babies were often given insufficient or the wrong food. They were expected to eat bread and meat at a very early age before their stomachs could manage it, and frequently died as a result.

Poor people struggling to earn a living could not cope with screaming babies who were hungry, uncomfortable or ill, so that the infants were doped with opium which could actually be bought in penny bottles at the chemists. Frequently the babies never woke from their drugged sleep.

The nineteenth century was a period of great drunkenness among the poor, and many babies died of sheer neglect, either because their parents did not realise what was happening to their family or else because the money that should have been spent on the children went on beer. Finally, there was the dreadful practice of baby farming. Parents who did not want to look after their children could take them to a woman who took in babies for a living and charged only five or ten pence a week. Dozens of neglected, unwanted infants would be crowded into a slum house, rarely washed, fed as little as possible and given no attention. The more that died, the better it was for the woman who ran the establishment.

If it had been only the 150 babies out of every 1,000 who died, it would have been bad enough, but unfortunately many of those who lived were stunted, deformed and sickly. When a big army recruiting campaign took place in 1899, it was found that 40 out of every 100 young men who volunteered were completely unfit even for the army's low standards, and had to be rejected. One of the greatest achievements of the twentieth century has been the reduction in the number of child deaths and the vast improvement in the health of the adult population which is a direct result of their healthier childhood.

---

1. What acts mentioned in this chapter helped to clean up the towns and improve health? Mention them by name and say what each aimed to do.
2. What advantages were there in being able to put someone to sleep before performing an operation?
3. Why is Florence Nightingale so important in the history of medicine and medical care? Find out about her work.
4. Look up Jenner in an encyclopaedia and then write about him briefly. What was his great contribution to medical science?
5. Why is it so important to have adequate sewage disposal?

8

NINETEENTH CENTURY EUROPE

Introduction

Except for the Napoleonic Wars (1793–1815) and the Crimean War (1854–6) Britain tried to remain as far as she could from the problems of Europe in the nineteenth century. She had quite enough worries of her own in building up her industry, her markets overseas and her empire to interfere more than was necessary in the affairs of her neighbours across the Channel.

But while Britain was digging more coal, manufacturing more goods, building more railways and ships, and developing her colonies, the rest of Europe was not idle. The twenty years of war that ended in 1815 had made sure that the old way of life had gone for ever in spite of the statesmen's efforts to put the clock back at the Congress of Vienna. The whole continent was searching, in different ways, for a new pattern of life to replace the one destroyed by Napoleon's armies.

There were five main lines of development and some countries followed all of them. There was the usual struggle for power and influence; there was a battle to unite all of the small states speaking the same language into one large state; there was a rise in feeling of pride in one's own country; there were searches for better forms of government in which the people as well as the nobles had a share, and towards the end of the century there was a rush to follow Britain's example of industrialisation.

Unfortunately one country cannot gain power, people and territory unless another loses so that the states were bound to come into conflict. Although some of these wars were sharp and bloody, none of them lasted very long or spread very far. The real struggles that were the results of the nineteenth century developments did not come until the twentieth century in the First and Second World Wars.

Europe at the end of the eighteenth century

This is a map of Europe as it appears today: at the end of the eighteenth century it was a very different place. Many of the countries we know did not exist and some of the others were very different. Only Spain, Portugal, France, Denmark, Switzerland and Britain had anything like the frontiers that we know today. Germany, for example, was a mass of over 300 small states, some no larger than a small town. Italy was divided into eleven separate kingdoms, while what is now Greece, Yugo-Slavia, Bulgaria and Rumania were part of the Turkish Empire. Austria, Czecho-Slovakia and Hungary, together with parts of the present Poland, formed the Austro-Hungarian Empire, while the rest of Poland was divided between Russia and Prussia.

France and Austria-Hungary were the most powerful of these states, but Britain, Prussia and Russia were rapidly growing in strength.

With a few strong states and a mass of small, weak ones there was always the temptation to fight and to seize some of the other tiny countries, but the statesmen tried to keep peace by what they called the Balance of Power. Normally the big states kept quite separate, but if one of them looked as if it were becoming too strong or if it formed an alliance with another, the remaining countries would band together to oppose it. If the two groups were equal they thought that neither side would be willing to start a war in case it was defeated.

In most countries of Europe conditions for the people were much as they had been in Britain in the middle ages. There were, on the whole, two classes of people—the rich and the peasants—though in the few towns there were a few merchants, lawyers and artisans who formed a tiny middle class. Kings ruled alone, advised as and when they wished by their councillors and courtiers, for very few countries had anything vaguely like a parliament, and in the few that did have some sort of assembly it was completely powerless. The French 'parliament' for example, did not meet between 1614 and 1789, a period of 175 years.

When a strong king was on the throne, most of the nobles were kept in some order: when there was a weak one, they did as they pleased. But strong king or weak, nobles peaceful or quarrelsome, the peasants knew that their fate would be much the same. Occasionally a strong king might try to improve the condition of his poorer subjects, but he always met with strong opposition from his nobles who felt that their position might be threatened, and who did their best to undo the king's reforms on his death.

The nobles generally lived lives of luxury and laziness, and enjoyed many privileges. They alone could hunt and fish, for example, and in many countries they paid no taxes. The peasants, on the other hand, especially in central and eastern Europe, were still serfs. They were their lord's possessions and could do nothing without his permission, nor,

116

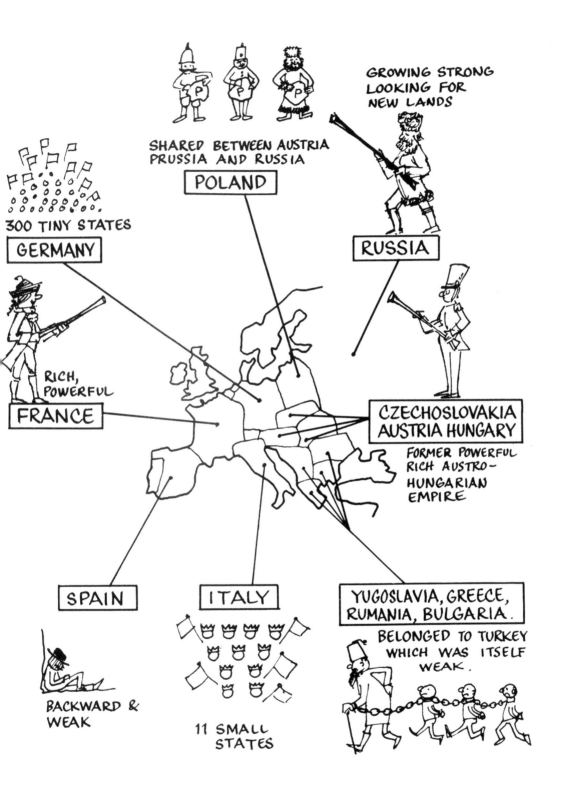

SHARED BETWEEN AUSTRIA
PRUSSIA AND RUSSIA

POLAND

GROWING STRONG
LOOKING FOR
NEW LANDS

300 TINY STATES

GERMANY

RUSSIA

RICH,
POWERFUL

FRANCE

CZECHOSLOVAKIA
AUSTRIA HUNGARY

FORMER POWERFUL
RICH AUSTRO-
HUNGARIAN
EMPIRE

SPAIN

ITALY

YUGOSLAVIA, GREECE,
RUMANIA, BULGARIA.

BELONGED TO TURKEY
WHICH WAS ITSELF
WEAK.

BACKWARD &
WEAK

11 SMALL
STATES

usually, without a payment to him. All they had to look for was harsh treatment by their masters, and constant squeezing for taxes by their lord, by the king and by the Church. It did not matter much whether one was a peasant in Russia, Poland, Austria or France because life was the same hard round of labour and poverty.

There were few towns in Europe and little industry. The few factories were operated by hand and controlled by groups of merchants and craftsmen whose ideas still belonged to the middle ages when the gild had been founded. All but a small minority of the population lived in villages or small towns and worked in agriculture, which was very primitive indeed. With so many peasants to do the drudgery the nobles had little need of better methods or machinery.

The average European took no pride in his country: if asked, he would be more likely to say he was Baron X's servant or the Marquis of Y's serf rather than an Austrian or a Frenchman. His country, in the shape of his king or his master, took his labour and his money and gave him little in return: why, therefore, should he feel strongly about being Russian or Hungarian or Italian? A good example of this is the way ordinary men were willing to fight for any country, even against their own homeland, if they were paid. Most of the wars of the period were fought between armies of hired men: even Britain 'bought' soldiers. During the American War of Independence, 1776–81, out of 35,000 troops fighting the colonists under the British flag, only 6,000 were British while the rest were mainly recruited from the German duchies of Ansbach, Brunswick and Hesse at a price per head of between £153 to £275.

One of the most important features of the nineteenth century is the awakening of the spirit of nationalism in Europe—that is, men learned to take a pride in their own country and were willing to fight and die for it.

The kings of Europe were often corrupt or stupid: the nobles often greedy, cruel and haughty; the peasants usually poor, ill-treated and down-trodden. Only the rich knew freedom, while life for the poor was several centuries behind. All of the ingredients for a great explosion were boiling up inside Europe.

---

1. Briefly explain what is meant by the phrase 'the balance of power'. Use your own words.
2. Explain why so little *national* feeling was to be found amongst the poorer classes in Europe. What caused this to change? Use your own words to explain.

SOME DIFFERENCE BETWEEN BRITAIN AND THE REST OF EUROPE IN 1780

MOST OF EUROPE	BRITAIN
KINGS RULED ABSOLUTELY	KINGS HAD RELATIVELY LITTLE POWER
NO PARLIAMENTS OR USELESS ONES	PARLIAMENT STRONG AND OUTSPOKEN
PEASANTS STILL SERFS & NOT FREE TO MOVE	SERFDOM ABOLISHED FOR 400 YEARS. PEASANTS FREED.
NO NATIONAL FEELING FOR OWN COUNTRY	STRONG PRIDE IN BRITAIN
PRIVILEGED NOBLES	PRIVILEGES & TAXES MORE EQUALLY SHARED
PRIMITIVE AGRICULTURE	IMPROVING AGRICULTURE

9

THE STORMY PATH OF FRANCE

The story of France from 1789 to 1899 is a wild one. In a single century she experienced three revolutions; two major wars, both of which she lost; several minor ones; six kings and a change from having a monarch to being a republic three times. And as if these political troubles were not enough, the country began the great upheaval of going through an industrial revolution as Britain had done.

Like most European countries in 1789 France was still much as Britain had been in the middle ages. There were, generally speaking, only two classes—the very rich and the very poor. The king and his court ruled absolutely: the French equivalent of parliament had not been called for 175 years so that, even though it had little power when it was sitting, the ordinary people had no way of expressing their point of view.

Many of the nobles lived at the court in Paris and allowed their estates to be run by harsh bailiffs who, together with the Church, squeezed as much money and labour out of the peasants as they could. The peasant was not allowed to hunt or fish; he was compelled to do military service; he was often forced to make roads and bridges; he had to pay taxes to the king, to his lord and to the church. To make matters worse, the tax collectors were usually dishonest and dragged twice as much from the poor as they should have done. The nobles, of course, were exempt from all these disagreeable duties.

All of this had gone on for centuries, and might have gone on longer, but during the eighteenth century a number of writers (especially Rousseau in France and Tom Paine in England) published books in which they said that all men were equal, and attacked the conditions which then existed in France.

The idea of revolution was thus sown in men's minds, but still they hesitated until the colonists in North America showed them the way. The apparently weak colonists rose against the powerful British in the American War of Independence in 1776 and set themselves free of the tyranny of their masters. The example was not lost on the French who, driven to desperation by a series of bad harvests which affected town and country alike, rose in revolt in 1789.

At first the revolution was fairly peaceful. Because the government was almost bankrupt, king Louis XVI was compelled to call parliament.

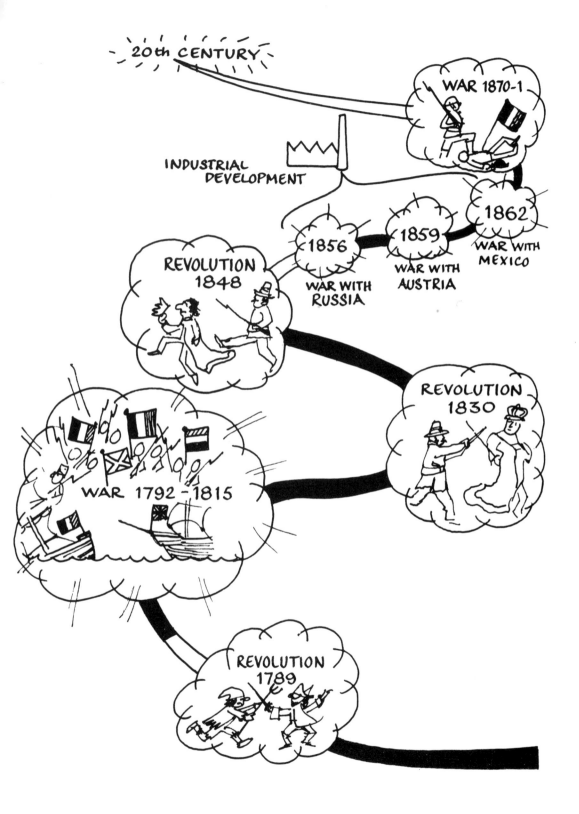

The ordinary people hoped that this would do something about their grievances, but when the meetings dragged on and on without any results, a ragged Paris mob attacked and captured the great prison, the Bastille. When they burst in they found only six prisoners, but the fall of the Bastille on July 14th, which is still a national holiday in France, was the signal for the revolution to begin in earnest.

Parliament, which was now under the influence of the mob, passed many laws which abolished the privileges of the nobles, reorganised taxation and cut down the power of the king and the Church. As yet there were no executions, but many aristocrats fled to neighbouring countries where they urged the rulers to make war on France to restore the nobles' property. Austria and Prussia in particular were only too eager to attack France for there was always the danger that if the ordinary people there gained the upper hand, the peasants in other countries might get rebellious ideas. So, expecting to defeat the rebels quickly and easily, they invaded France in 1792.

The French responded by calling on all peasants in all countries to rise against their masters, and promised that in any territory they captured the kings would be abolished and the rule of the people set up.

By 1793 Britain, Holland, Spain and Sardinia had joined the war to put down the revolutionaries, while in France itself a group of extreme men had taken over the government. To divert attention from the war they began the Reign of Terror, and in the next fifteen months about 20,000 people, including the king and queen, many aristocrats and clergymen and most of the original leaders of the revolution were executed on the guillotine.

Christianity was abolished and the worship of reason was set up. In order to break completely with the old way of life a new calendar in which the year 1 was the year of the fall of the Bastille was introduced, and the names of the days and months were replaced by new, revolutionary ones. All titles such as 'duke', 'marquis' and 'prince' were dropped and everyone, regardless of rank, was called 'citizen'.

In spite of the brutality of the years 1793–5 much good work was done by the revolutionary government. A system of education was planned, old laws were brought up to date, schemes for looking after the poor and aged were introduced and the metric system of metres and kilograms replaced the complicated weights and measures then in use.

Meanwhile the war against France had spread, but the European kings, who had thought it would be so easy to defeat the mob, discovered that the French had found a new spirit. For the first time they were fighting for their own freedom and not for a master. They knew that if they lost this fight there would be a return to the old order, if not to an even worse one. Everywhere the enemy was stopped and then, led by a young officer, Napoleon Bonaparte, the citizen armies of France went over to the attack. By 1797 Holland, Spain, Austria, Italy and Prussia had surrendered and Britain was left alone. Fortunately the British navy had been able to beat all the fleets sent against it and so saved England from invasion.

The French armies next turned their eyes towards India, and after capturing Malta, sailed on to Egypt. At first they were as successful here as they had been in Europe, but in 1798 a British fleet under Lord Nelson caught the French navy by surprise at anchor near Alexandria and destroyed it. Napoleon himself abandoned his army and escaped to Europe, where, taking heart at Britain's success, Russia and Prussia again declared war. Both were soundly beaten again by the seemingly invincible French, and thoroughly weary of fighting, the countries of Europe signed a peace treaty which everyone knew was really only a half-time break (1802–3).

When the war began again Napoleon was determined to conquer Britain. Besides planning the usual invasion by sea he also considered digging a tunnel under the Channel and sending his army across in a fleet of balloons. Fortunately both of these schemes were impracticable at the time, and the invasion by sea was prevented by the great naval victory at Trafalgar, where Nelson finally disposed of the French and Spanish fleets.

Nelson's plan of battle at Trafalgar.

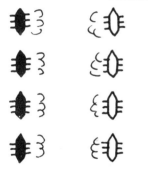

In traditional naval battles the ships of the two fleets sailed in parallel lines firing broadsides at each other until one side or other was so badly damaged that it could be boarded.

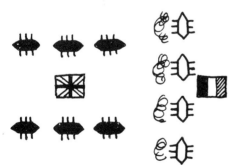

Nelson's plan was to sail in two columns straight at the French line. This meant that for several hours as he was approaching Nelson could not fire at the French while they could fire at him. It was a risky plan for the British fleet could have been destroyed before it reached the French line.

123

When the British ships did reach the French line they could fire at point-blank range from both sides while the French could not easily reply. The French line was completely broken up and the ship-to-ship fighting began. The tactics were completely successful.

The land war now flared up again with the bulk of fighting in Spain and Portugal between the French, and the British who were led by Sir Arthur Wellesley, later to become Duke of Wellington.

In 1812 Napoleon made his greatest mistake. Turning eastwards he led an army of over half a million men into Russia. Cold, hunger, disease, wild animals and above all, Russian guerillas attacked the Grand Army continuously on the dreadful 1,500 mile march to Moscow. As soon as Napoleon tried to fight a pitched battle his enemy just vanished into the endless forest, often destroying all the wheat and driving away all the livestock. In the nineteenth century an invading army had no lorries or trains to bring up food supplies, and had to live on what it could find in the countryside through which it was passing. The desperately hungry army struggled on to Moscow where it hoped to find both food and shelter from the bitter winter, but Napoleon found it in flames. There was nothing he could do but retreat, with all his enemies of the outward journey attacking more fiercely. When the Grand Army finally tottered back to France, nine of every ten men who had begun the journey were lost.

At last the sheer weight of numbers began to tell as Russia, Prussia and Austria joined Britain once again. In 1814 Napoleon was defeated and sent to live in exile on the island of Elba. But while the allies were discussing what should happen to the mess left by twenty years of war, Napoleon escaped, landed in France and managed to muster yet another army. After some successes, however, he faced the British and Prussians at Waterloo in 1815, and the long struggle was over. Napoleon surrendered to a British ship (he said that it was really the navy which had defeated him) and spent the rest of his life on the lonely island of St. Helena in mid-Atlantic.

In 1815 the important statesmen of Europe met at the Congress of Vienna in Austria to decide what was to be done with France and the other countries whose life had been so disturbed by the wars. Unfortunately the Congress decided that as far as possible it would restore things as they had been in 1789. Although many nations had tasted freedom for the first time, and although the ideas of the French Revolution had spread, the old kings and their governments were placed again in power. Trouble was bound to follow, and you can read in Chapters 10 and 11 how this happened in Italy and Germany. However, in one way at least the Congress of Vienna was a success, for there was no major war in Europe for a century afterwards.

The story of France for the rest of the century is one of change and of a search for the right form of government. The brothers of the executed Louis XVI ruled in turn, Louis XVIII from 1814 to 1824 and Charles X from 1824–30. Louis, remembering all that had happened, stepped very carefully with his government, but Charles, feeling more secure, began to be more and more strict.

At last, when Charles refused to accept an election in 1830 which returned to parliament a number of members who disagreed with him, the people of Paris rebelled. It was not the bloodthirsty affair of 1789, but the streets were barricaded with overturned carts and sandbags. When the army mutinied and went over to the side of the people, Charles abdicated and a new king, Louis Philippe, Duke of Orleans was chosen.

Louis set himself up as a 'citizen' king and mixed with the ordinary people much more than any previous monarch of France. Yet even in this he did not succeed for the French themselves did not really know what they wanted. In 1848 when the wave of revolutions swept through Europe the barricades once more went up in the streets of Paris, and a short but sharp battle raged between the mob and the police and army. Louis Philippe abdicated, and travelling as a Mr William Smith, he reached England where he spent the rest of his life. The French people had now had enough of kings for a while, and for a second time tried a republic. This time it lasted four years, when another man, Napoleon's nephew, managed to have himself elected as Emperor Napoleon III. This new Napoleon was reasonably successful: he allowed the people to choose a parliament (which had no power at all really) and began to reform all aspects of French life. Roads and railways were built, and industry flourished; there was a successful small war against Russia and a less successful one against Mexico. Life in France for eighteen years moved fairly gaily, smoothly and prosperously—until the un-expected and humiliating defeat by the German army in 1871 (see Chapter 10).

The war of 1870–1 was the first in which flying machines were used seriously. When Paris was besieged gas filled balloons were used to fly out letters and important people and also to drop leaflets on the encircling Prussian troops. As the balloons could not fly back into the capital, each one carried a basket of carrier pigeons. If the 'pilot' was able to land in an area not captured by the Germans he sent on the mail and then had the return letters photographed on very small film which was

GERMAN TROOPS

PARIS

fastened to the birds' legs. In five months sixty-six balloons carrying nearly two hundred passengers and three million letters slipped out of the trapped city.

Although the siege lasted less than five months there was terrible hardship in the city, especially about food. Here are some prices (at approximately today's figure) which were being paid after about three months.

Butter	—	£8 a lb.
Eggs	—	40p each.
Cat	—	£1·50 a lb.
Rat	—	30p each.

When all of the horses, dogs and cats had gone, the animals in the zoos were slaughtered and sold to those who could afford them. Elephant fetched about £9 a pound, but the hippopotamus was saved because no one would pay the £16,000 asked for it!

Once more the French were ready for a change; Napoleon was swept away and the Third Republic formed. This lasted until it was defeated by Hitler in 1940.

For the last quarter of the century France steadily forged ahead with industrialisation, with one eye steadily fixed on Germany. The defeat of 1871 and the loss of Alsace and Lorraine, which Germany seized as part of her victory, never ceased to rankle in every Frenchman's heart, and everyone knew that sooner or later France would try to gain her revenge.

---

1. Write a short account of France's stormy century. Make sure that you explain why the French people rebelled in 1789, how successful they were and why it took a long time for the country to settle down after the 'Terror'.
2. With history books and encyclopaedias find out what you can about *one* of the following and write as much about him as you can: (*a*) Napoleon I, (*b*) Earl Nelson, (*c*) the Duke of Wellington.

France and her rivals in 1899.

EXPORT EARNINGS   IMPORTS

A century of wars and revolutions had left France much less developed industrially than Britain or Germany.

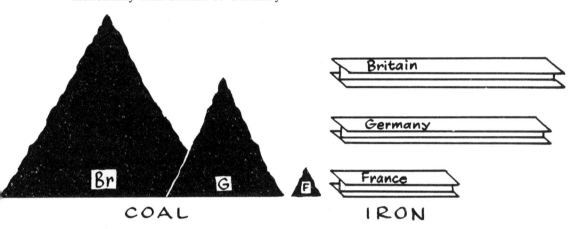

COAL   IRON

GERMANY   FRANCE   BRITAIN

ARMIES

10

THE GROWTH OF GERMANY

At the beginning of the nineteenth century Germany, as we know it, did not exist. In 1815 it consisted of over 200 separate states of all sizes. Easily the largest and most powerful was Prussia, but there were half a dozen like Hanover and Bavaria of medium size, and almost two hundred small ones, some of them no larger than a small town. Big or little, each state had its own ruler, whether king, prince, duke or bishop, and its own laws and its own customs duties. All, however, spoke the German language which helped considerably when they joined together. This division pleased France and Austria, who were the leading continental European countries, for as long as Germany was divided, she was weak.

The first steps towards union came in a small way between 1816 and 1849 when many of the states, led by Prussia, joined what they called a *Zollverein* or customs union. Although each country kept its own ruler and laws the customs duties on each other's goods were made the same and gradually reduced so that trading became much easier. In the eight years between 1834 and 1842 the exports and imports of the states belonging to the *Zollverein* doubled, and members began to wonder if it would not be a good idea to unite for other things as well. Apart from some unrest and minor rebellions however, little further development took place until 1861.

In that year, as had happened in Sardinia and Piedmont some years earlier when Victor Emmanuel and Count Cavour came to power, Prussia had a new king and a new prime minister. These two men, the ambitious William I and the even more ambitious Otto von Bismarck, were to change the whole history of Germany, of Europe and of the world. Bismarck especially was determined to see Prussia leading Germany, and Germany leading Europe, and thirty years later when he was dismissed, his dream had almost come true. From being a loose group of states among the most backward in western Europe, the new united and industrial Germany had emerged, and was able between 1914 and 1918 to fight and almost defeat the combined armies of Britain, France, Belgium, Russia, Italy and the United States.

Bismarck could see that the German people could not have two leaders: it had to be either Prussia or Austria, and he was determined

FRANCE WEAK

1871- GERMAN EMPIRE SET UP WITH WILLIAM OF PRUSSIA AS EMPEROR

AUSTRIA WEAK

1870-1 PRUSSIA DEFEATS FRANCE

AUSTRIA WEAK

FRANCE WORRIED BY PRUSSIA'S GROWING POWER

1866- NORTH GERMAN CONFEDERATION

AUSTRIA NOW WEAK

FRANCE DELIGHTED

1866- PRUSSIA DEFEATS AUSTRIA IN 7 WEEKS WAR

18 61 BISMARCK, PRIME MINISTER

FRANCE

1816-1849 ZOLLVEREIN

AUSTRIA

FRANCE

GERMANY-200 STATES, WEAK

AUSTRIA

that it should be Prussia. Accordingly, in 1864, he invited the unsuspecting Emperor of Austria to help him fight Denmark over two small states called Schleswig and Holstein. The war lasted only a few days, but as Bismarck had planned right from the beginning, Prussia and Austria could not agree on how to rule the lands they had captured. This gave Bismarck the excuse to turn on his allies and in the Seven Weeks' War he utterly defeated the Austrian Army.

Napoleon III, Emperor of France, was well pleased at first, for now that Austria was weak, his greatest rival had gone. When, however, as a result of Bismarck's victory all the states of the northern half of Germany joined Prussia in the North German Confederation under William I, Napoleon felt a little suspicious.

And France's suspicions were well founded, for she was next on the list of Bismarck's victims. The Prussians knew that the states of southern Germany would not join their confederation unless they thought they were in danger of being attacked by France. Bismarck knew that it would be of no help to him if HE declared war: somehow he had to make France begin the fighting so that he could act as if he were rescuing the south Germans.

The chance came in 1868 when the queen of Spain was turned off the throne. Bismarck, probably by bribery, managed to get Prince Leopold, a relative of William I, accepted as the next king. France was very angry, of course, knowing full well the danger of having two kings of the same family on two of her frontiers, and objected at once. William I, a sincere man, saw their point and withdrew Prince Leopold's claim to the Spanish throne. Bismarck was dismayed, for he saw all of his plans collapsing.

The French, who considered they had won a great victory, tried to humble William by asking him to promise never to allow Leopold's name to be put forward again. William good naturedly refused to do this, and his actual words were sent by telegram to Bismarck who was on the point of resigning. The cunning prime minister now saw his opportunity, and at what we might today call a press conference he published a brilliantly worded fake telegram which at the same time was a terrible insult to France and also made the German people feel that it was they who had been insulted.

The French felt so deeply that they declared war, but while their badly-led troops were merely planning to attack southern Germany, the Prussians swept into France, captured three armies and took the emperor prisoner.

Although some resistance was organised in the south of France, the Germans swept on to Paris which they besieged for four months before it surrendered.

Under the peace treaty France was forced to give up the two 'counties' of Alsace and Lorraine to the Germans, to pay £200,000,000 and to

How Germany's rate of increase outstripped that of her rivals.

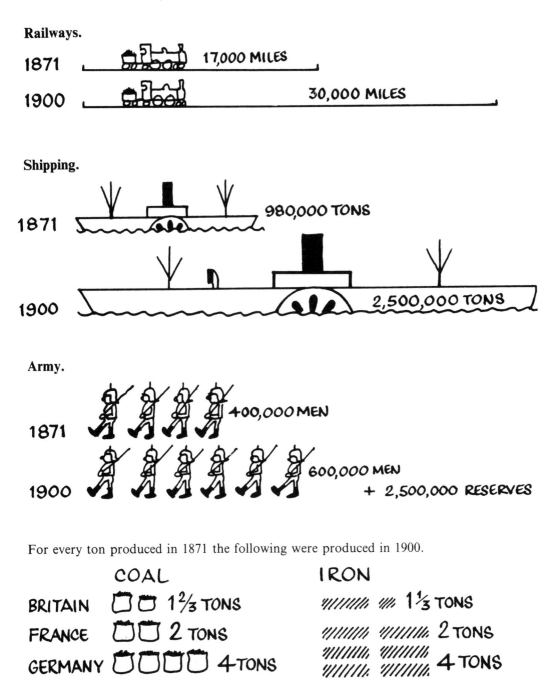

Railways.

1871 — 17,000 MILES

1900 — 30,000 MILES

Shipping.

1871 — 980,000 TONS

1900 — 2,500,000 TONS

Army.

1871 — 400,000 MEN

1900 — 600,000 MEN + 2,500,000 RESERVES

For every ton produced in 1871 the following were produced in 1900.

	COAL	IRON
BRITAIN	1⅔ TONS	1⅓ TONS
FRANCE	2 TONS	2 TONS
GERMANY	4 TONS	4 TONS

suffer the humiliation of having German soldiers in the country until the debt had been paid in full.

The southern states of Germany now saw that they must join the Prussians, and in 1871 the German Empire was set up with William I of Prussia as Emperor and Bismarck as its Imperial Chancellor. The whole of Germany was now one, and could devote itself to rapid industrialisation. In the last thirty years of the century progress was phenomenal. Industry, especially coal mining, iron and steel, armaments, transport and chemicals shot ahead at a pace never seen before in history. In one thing only was the new Germany disappointed—by the time she was united almost all of the colonies in Africa, South America and the East had been seized by Britain, France, Belgium and Holland so that there was little left worth having for Germany. Bismarck wanted not only to be a leading European power, he also wanted to be a leading world power, and much of German industry was directed to the war which must sooner or later break out. All through the last years of the century Germany and France raced neck and neck to build bigger and bigger armies and stocks of weapons, while Germany and Britain raced to build bigger fleets of battleships. The war in which these weapons were used did not come in the nineteenth century, but the twentieth had to wait only fourteen years before Germany made the first of her two terrible attempts to become the greatest nation on earth.

---

1. In your own words describe how Germany became a powerful State.
2. What did Bismarck do to make Germany so powerful a country? Why was it so important to knit the States together?
3. With the aid of an encyclopaedia find out what you can about Otto von Bismarck and write a brief biography.

11

ITALY BECOMES A NATION
1859-1870

As we have seen, at the beginning of the nineteenth century parts of Europe were not single countries as they are now, but were made up of many small states, each ruled by its own king, queen or duke. Italy in 1789 was made up of about a dozen such states, the northern ones under the influence of Austria and the southern ones under the influence of Spain.

When Napoleon conquered Italy between 1802 and 1809 he joined these small states into three larger ones which were much more efficiently run, and suggested that sooner or later the Italian people should be one nation.

At the Congress of Vienna, however, the statesmen merely split up Italy into about a dozen parts once more and handed the kingdoms back to their old rulers. The Italians were bitterly disappointed and very angry, and for the next thirty years there were small revolutions breaking out in one state after another. Each time the army of either Austria or France was called in to put down the rebellion, so that by 1849 things seemed very much as they had been sixty years earlier. But in fact, things were not quite the same, for each defeat by a foreign army only made the Italian people more determined to unite their country.

In 1849 a remarkable man was crowned king of the twin kingdoms of Sardinia and Piedmont in the north of Italy, and three years later he appointed an even more remarkable man, Count Cavour, as his prime minister. Cavour, whose mind planned the whole of the operation of uniting Italy, could see that tiny Sardinia could never overthrow mighty Austria without help, and by cunning statesmanship he persuaded Napoleon III, Emperor of France, to become his ally.

After a short, but very sharp war which ended with the defeat of the Austrians at the battle of Solferino, the state of Lombardy was added to Sardinia. Although the rest of northern Italy was still in the hands of the Austrians, Napoleon refused to continue the fight, partly because he was genuinely horrified by the dreadful slaughter of soldiers in the battle.

But if Napoleon was horrified, a wealthy Swiss merchant named Henri Dunant was even more appalled. Happening to pass the battle-field and seeing the agony of the wounded and the brutal way in which they were treated, he campaigned for an organisation that would help suffering wherever it happened, regardless of race. As a result of his efforts the International Red Cross was born in Geneva which is still its head-quarters. Its emblem is in fact the Swiss flag in reverse.

Four states in Central Italy were so impressed by the Sardinians that Cavour was able to persuade their rulers to join him and to accept Victor Emmanuel as their king. Two other states in the centre needed an invasion and defeat in battle to persuade them to join.

Now only three parts of the country did not belong to the growing state of Italy. In the north-east was Venice, still strongly held by the Austrian army; in the centre was the land round Rome which was ruled by the Pope, and in the south was the largest of the remaining kingdoms, Naples and the island of Sicily. These were ruled by a very harsh king, Francis.

In 1860 a small rebellion broke out in Sicily and a famous guerilla leader named Garibaldi hurried southwards. Although Victor Emmanuel dare not give him help openly as this would be supporting a revolution against a brother king, he did give Garibaldi a large sum of money from his own pocket for arms, and Cavour's government pretended not to notice that men from Sardinia slipped away to fight. At the head of a ragged band of volunteers—his Redshirts—Garibaldi fought and defeated the army of the king of Naples, and in three months he was master of the island. He then set out for the mainland, where his amazing victories continued. In another six months Garibaldi was dictator of the whole of southern Italy as well, but when he met Victor Emmanuel he handed over all power to the king. The two men rode side by side into Naples, and though Garibaldi could have had anything he asked from the grateful Italians, he refused all rewards and slipped away to live in poverty on the barren island where he had made his home. This is how the famous historian G. M. Trevelyan described it in his book *Garibaldi and the making of Italy*.

"In the last two days Victor Emmanuel had offered him an estate for Menotti [Garibaldi's son], the title of King's aide-de-camp for his younger son, a dowry for his daughter, a royal castle and a steamer for himself. But he had refused them all. His secretary, Basso, had borrowed a few hundred francs of papermoney from a friend, for necessary expenses. He himself had stowed on board the *Washington* [the boat which was taking him back to his island] a bag of seed corn for his farm. With these spoils the steamer, almost unobserved, left port at break of day.

He was soon back at his old daily occupation of man's primitive struggle with nature. . . . Again the dawn and the twilight on the Straits of Bonifacio saw him at work among the granite boulders, industriously putting seed into the scrapings of earth which he called

134

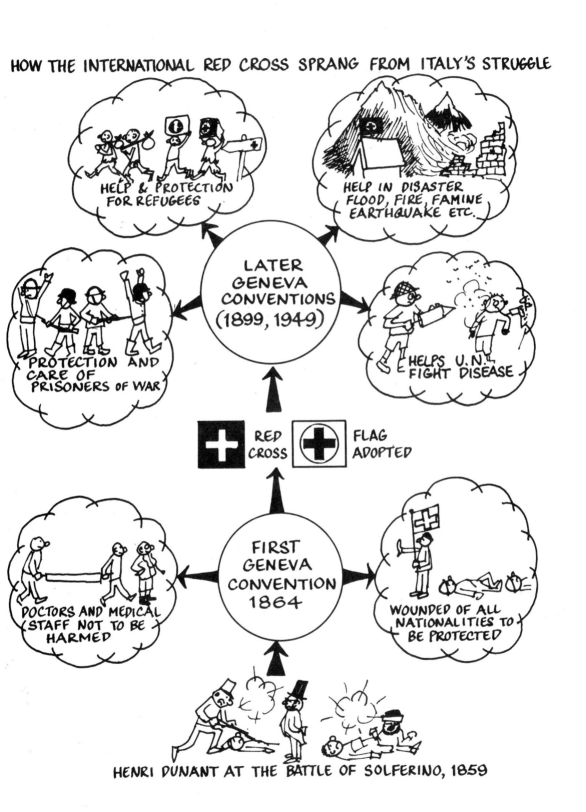

HOW THE INTERNATIONAL RED CROSS SPRANG FROM ITALY'S STRUGGLE

HELP & PROTECTION FOR REFUGEES

HELP IN DISASTER FLOOD, FIRE, FAMINE EARTHQUAKE ETC.

LATER GENEVA CONVENTIONS (1899, 1949)

PROTECTION AND CARE OF PRISONERS OF WAR

HELPS U.N. FIGHT DISEASE

RED CROSS   FLAG ADOPTED

FIRST GENEVA CONVENTION 1864

DOCTORS AND MEDICAL STAFF NOT TO BE HARMED

WOUNDED OF ALL NATIONALITIES TO BE PROTECTED

HENRI DUNANT AT THE BATTLE OF SOLFERINO, 1859

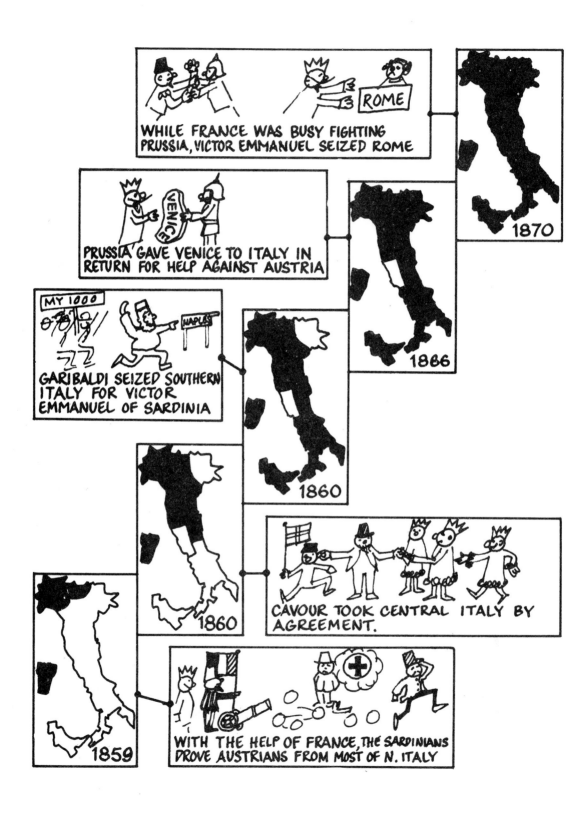

his fields; sheltering a few sad vines from the sweeping winds of the straits; calling up his cows by name from their pasturage among the wild, odorous brushwood; and seeking the strayed goats on the precipice top."

Except for the two small areas, all of Italy was now united, and Victor Emmanuel and Cavour had not long to wait for the last pieces of their jig-saw to drop in place. In 1866 Italy fought on Prussia's side against her old enemy Austria, and at Austria's defeat she was given Venice as a reward. It was now only fear of France, which was a strongly Catholic country, that prevented the king from seizing the Pope's territory, but when in 1870 France was locked in a desperate struggle with Prussia, his chance came. Victor Emmanuel marched into Rome, which became the capital of a now completely united Italy.

---

1. Show simply how Cavour succeeded in uniting Italy. Use your own words where possible.
2. With the aid of an encyclopaedia find out all you can about Garibaldi and write a brief biography.
3. Look up *Henri Dunant,* and *International Red Cross* in an encyclopaedia, then write a brief essay about them. You could, if you wished, make a class exhibition project of it, by collecting stories and photographs, making drawings and writing connecting notes linking the earliest days of the Red Cross with its present work and scope. (The British Red Cross Society's headquarters are at 14 Grosvenor Crescent, London, W.1.).

12

THE 19th CENTURY
A PICTURE SUMMARY

Here are some differences in the life and work of people living in 1800, 1900 and today.

1800	1900	TODAY
THE TOTAL POPULATION OF BRITAIN WAS ABOUT...		
10 MILLION	35 MILLION	56 MILLION
IF YOU REACHED THE AGE OF 1, YOU COULD EXPECT TO LIVE TO THE AGE OF...		
About 40 - 50	53 56	69 72
OF EVERY 10 PEOPLE, THESE LIVED IN THE TOWN AND COUNTRY...		
AN AVERAGE CLASS OF 30 BOYS WOULD FIND JOBS IN THE FOLLOWING OCCUPATIONS...		
FARMING		
INDUSTRY		
OTHERS		

These drawings show some of the great changes in people's lives during the 19th century.

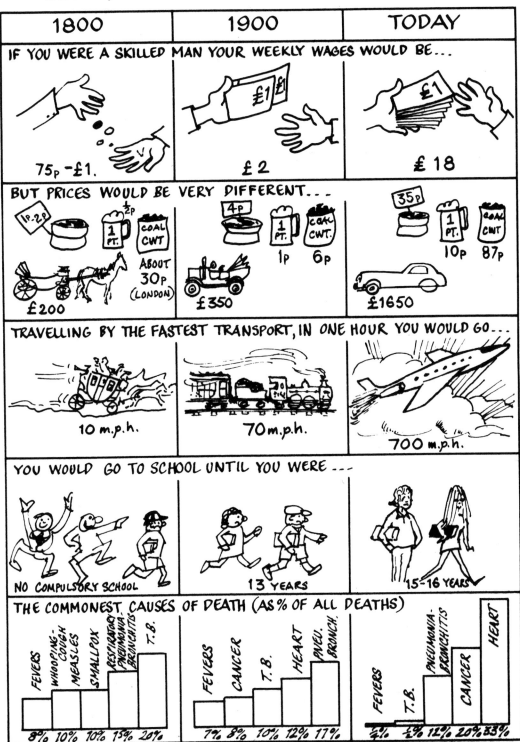

1800	1850	1900

THE LATEST STYLE IN WEALTHY MEN'S HOUSES...

... AND IN FURNITURE

A TOWN MIGHT OFFER THESE ADVANTAGES...

CANDLES
WELLS
MUDDY UNLIT STREETS

GAS JET
PIPE IN STREET
MAIN STREETS PAVED & GAS LIT

GAS OR ELECTRIC
MOST STREETS PAVED AND LIT BY GAS OR ELECTRICITY

THESE WOULD HAVE BEEN THE MAIN PASTIMES...

CRICKET
RACING
BULL BAITING
COCK FIGHTING
PRIZEFIGHTING

FOOTBALL & RUGBY
ROLLER SKATING
ATHLETICS
SEA BATHING

BOXING

THESE WOULD HAVE BEEN THE MAIN CHANGES IN FOOD...

BREAD CHEESE MEAT AND VEGETABLES – ALL HOME PREPARED

MORE –
BUTTER
FISH
MILK
MUSTARD
SOUP POWDER
A FEW PREPARED FOODS

N.Z
FROZEN MEAT
SOME TINNED FOOD
MORE PACKETS – CUSTARD CEREALS ETC.
FOREIGN FRUIT

FOR FURTHER READING

(* before a book means that it is more difficult, but still worth looking at.)

GENERAL

* * *The Age of Reform.* Sir L. Woodward. Oxford University Press.
* * *England 1870–1914.* Sir R. Ensor. Oxford University Press.
* * *History of the Homeland.* Henry Hamilton. Allen and Unwin.
* * *Early Victorian England.* Ed. G. M. Young. OUP.
* * *Victorian England: Portrait of an Age.* G. M. Young. OUP.
* *Human Documents of the Victorian Golden Age.* E. Royston Pike. Allen and Unwin.
* *A History of Everyday Things.* M. and C. H. B. Quennell. Batsford.
* *A Century of Change 1837–Today.* R. J. Unstead. A. & C. Black.
* *An Economic History of England 1066–1874.* C. M. Waters. OUP.
* *Picture Source Books for Social History.* Ed. M. Harrison. Allen and Unwin.
  Early nineteenth century; Late nineteenth century.

INDUSTRIAL LIFE AND COMMUNICATIONS

* *Human Documents of the Industrial Revolution.* E. Royston Pike. Allen and Unwin.
* * *The Bleak Age*
* * *The Town Labourer* } J. L. and B. Hammond. Longmans.
* * *The Skilled Labourer*
* * *A History of Technology.* Charles Singer and others. OUP.
  Vol. 4 1750–1850.
  Vol. 5 1850–1900.
* *A Short History of Technology.* Derry and Williams. OUP.
* *The Industrial Revolution 1760–1860.* M. E. Beggs Humphreys. Allen and Unwin.
* *Industry and Technology.* W. H. Chaloner and A. Musson. Visual History series. Vista.
* *Methuen's Outlines Series.*
  The Growth of Mechanical Power.
  Forge and Foundry.
  Coal Mines and Miners.
  Spinning and Weaving.
* *Changing Shape of Things Series.* Murray.
  Travel by Land.
  Travel by Sea.
  Travel by Air.
* *Transport.* J. Simmons. Visual Histories series. Vista.
* *The Story of Passenger Transport in Britain.* J. Joyce. Ian Allen.
* *British Canals: An Illustrated History.* Charles Hadfield. David and Charles.

141

PARLIAMENT, REFORMS AND TRADE UNIONS

Our Parliament. S. Gordon. Hansard Society.

The Vote 1832–1928. Jackdaw series. Cape.

Early Trade Unions. Jackdaw series. Cape.

Strike or Bargain? Today is History series. Blond Educational.

Social Reformers. N. Wymer. OUP.

Eminent Victorians. Lytton Strachey. Chatto and Windus. (Florence Nightingale, Dr. Arnold, Cardinal Manning.)

* *A Short History of the British Working Class Movement, 1789–1947.* G. D. H. Cole. Allen and Unwin.

SOCIAL LIFE

The Town. G. Martin. Visual Histories series. Vista.

Changing shape of Things series. Murray.

   Dress. James Laver.

   Houses. M. and A. Potter.

Today is History series. Blond Educational.

   I swear and Vow. (Medicine).

The Victorian Home, 1837–1901. R. Dutton. Batsford.

* *A Short History of Medicine.* Charles Singer. OUP.

Sports and Pastimes through the Ages. P. Moss. Harrap.

Meals through the Ages. P. Moss. Harrap.

Handbook of English Costume in the nineteenth century. C. W. & P. Cunningham. Faber.

Our Mothers. A. Bott and Irene Clephane. Gollancz.

Our Fathers. A. Bott. Heinemann.

   (Victorian magazine pictures of all aspects of social life.)

EUROPE

* *A History of Europe.* H. A. L. Fisher. Arnold.

* *A Short History of Germany 1815–1945.* E. J. Passant. Cambridge University Press.

The French Revolution. Editors of 'Horizon' magazine and D. L. Dowd. Cassell Caravel books.

The French Revolution. Arthur Booth. Muller 'True' books.

With Garibaldi in Italy. Godfrey Lias. Muller.

INDEX